Intention Obsession

Intention
Obsession

Rituals and Witchcraft
for Every Season

Erica Feldmann

HARVEST

An Imprint of WILLIAM MORROW

INTENTION OBSESSION. Copyright © 2025 by Erica Feldmann. All rights reserved. Printed in Canada. No part of this book may be used or reproduced in any manner whatsoever without written permission except in the case of brief quotations embodied in critical articles and reviews. For information, address HarperCollins Publishers, 195 Broadway, New York, NY 10007.

HarperCollins books may be purchased for educational, business, or sales promotional use. For information, please email the Special Markets Department at SPsales@harpercollins.com.

FIRST EDITION

Designed by Tai Blanche

Photography by Christy Czajkowski

Zodiac icons throughout © Юлия Мальцева/stock.adobe.com

Gradient backgrounds: pages i, ii, iii, vi, vii © Nattapol_Sritongcom/stock.adobe.com; pages iv, v, x–xxi, 227–282 © kastanka/stock.adobe.com; pages xviii, 26, 117 © fim.design/stock.adobe.com; pages 7–9 © Salman/stock.adobe.com; pages 49, 51, 60–61 © winterbee/stock.adobe.com; pages 73–74 © Ripi Art/stock.adobe.com; pages 124, 196, 205 © stigmatize/stock.adobe.com; pages 154–156 © Thapanawat/stock.adobe.com; pages 166–167, 173, 174–176 © Amona HD/stock.adobe.com; pages 224–229 © avextra/stock.adobe.com; pages 237–240, 250 © PhatCha/stock.adobe.com.

Library of Congress Cataloging-in-Publication Data has been applied for.

ISBN 978-0-06-335333-6

25 26 27 28 29 TC 10 9 8 7 6 5 4 3 2 1

For Lois and Barbara

Contents

Introduction

Greetings from Witch City! My name is Erica Feldmann and I am the founder of a store in Salem, Massachusetts, called HausWitch Home + Healing and the author of *HausMagick: Transform Your Home with Witchcraft*. I have been helping folks bring magick into their everyday lives for over ten years now and I've taken a lot of notes along the way. One thing that has become very clear to me over the years is that no matter what spell you cast, or what tools you use, the single most important ingredient is *intention*.

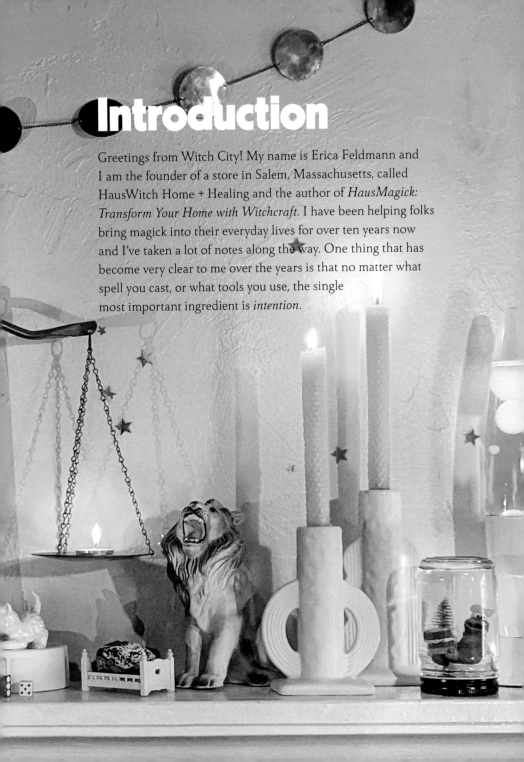

To me, intention is basically just thought + action. Living your life with intention is the opposite of being on autopilot. It can look like stirring your pot a certain number of times in a particular direction. It can look like a rhyme you made up to help you remember something. It can also look like thoughtfully choosing between five different kinds of Funfetti frosting at the supermarket to make your wife's boxed birthday cake into a spell. It can look like any or all of the ideas in this book. Your only task is to find ways to add intention to your life that feel most easeful. Dare I say, pleasurable. I don't think spirituality has to be painful or shameful. I think it can be quiet, private, and fun. Plus, I bet you're already doing it.

Here are some examples of what "intention" can and will look like in this book:

- Cleaning your space
- Making your bed
- Charming your grooming products
- Incorporating color into your decision-making process
- Factoring in the deities associated with the day of the week when scheduling things
- Planning a meal
- Using aromatherapy
- Pulling a tarot card
- Taking a nap

If none of those things sound too scary for you, then great! You're gonna love this book! Intention is a huge part of practicing magick, so you're halfway to being a very powerful magician just by acknowledging that.

This idea—of giving ourselves permission to honor what brings us joy, makes us feel powerful (as long as it doesn't harm yourself or anyone else, of course), and feels sacred to *us*, even if it seems silly or childlike or vulnerable—is a huge part of this book. I would love for you, dear reader, to learn to stretch the very powerful muscle that is your intuition and let it guide you through the creation of a more alive, magickal, and intentional life.

It is not lost on me that books like this are usually written by the folks with the most access to things like self-care, time off from work, health care, therapy, disposable income, and "little treats" in general. This book is no exception. Don't get me wrong, I am by no means swimming in cash like Scrooge McDuck and I have *lots* of student loan debt. But I also own my own home and business, have money in savings, and take very good care of myself where "little treats" are concerned. I acknowledge

that not everyone has those privileges, and so I put a lot of effort into designing these rituals so that most anyone could do them without expending enormous amounts of time, money, or energy if they don't have it to spare.

I've learned as the owner of a witch shop that some people don't want to be told that the magick is already inside of them. Capitalism and organized religion have disempowered people to the point where they just want to be told what to do, what to buy, and how to use it when it comes to magick and witchcraft. They trust outside sources more than they trust themselves. This is not the point of this book. I don't want to tell you how to live or make magick, but I want to give you some ideas. My big goals are just to help you use your feelings, develop your intuition, stay present, connect with the natural rhythm of the seasons, and

distract you from the mundane tedium of modern life.

I can also tell you that I do not practice a kind of magick that is measured in quantitative results. I practice a kind of magick designed to bring me peace and fulfillment. I don't often cast spells for money or love. I cast spells for abundance and self-worth. When I do cast a manifesting spell, I do so with the full knowledge that I am in co-creation with the universe and have no way of knowing if what I am trying to manifest is aligned with the highest and best outcome for me and my wider web of connections. Therefore if I don't get what I am trying to manifest, I don't see it as a failure but rather as a clue that the thing I was trying to manifest isn't actually right for me. To me, being a powerful witch means staying in alignment with my power, and that has more to do with how I feel than with the results of the spells I cast. If my

head isn't filled with negative self-talk or voices from my past that do not serve my best interests, it's much easier to feel the universe's gentle nudges helping me navigate the way forward. If I'm riddled with anxiety about being productive, I won't be able to sense that my body needs me to prioritize rest *in order to be* productive. If I'm ignoring how my own higher consciousness wants to guide me, how will I even know what spells to cast?

As you go through this book, you will see that some tough topics will come up. That is because this book is not based in a fantasy world and therefore cannot be all love and light and pretty ice cubes. (Although there *will* actually be pretty ice cubes, I promise!)

Our world is mediated by three forces that we can't move forward without acknowledging: capitalism, patriarchy, and white supremacy. No matter how you might feel about these concepts (hopefully you already hate them!), the facts are facts. Capitalism is the global economic order and it, by nature, exploits people for their labor. Patriarchy has been in place for thousands of years, and it prioritizes (to put it mildly) the power, desires, and entitlement of men. White supremacy, the reprehensible idea that white people should dominate society, has insidiously worked its way into so many facets of contemporary life that a lot of people can't even see around it. It can all feel very scary, especially for those whose identity puts them in the intersections of those things.

But here's the thing. Witches can confront what's scary, dark, bad, and sad. Because as witches, we know that we hold the power to transform and transmute. So rather than avoid these topics in order to avoid despair, anger, disenchantment, and so on, we're going to face them head on. Each chapter will provide practical ways to push back on these forces to reclaim your own personal sovereignty and engage with your community in powerful and productive ways. In some cases "community" will mean your friend group, and in some cases it will mean the whole human race and beyond! Either way, I hope that this book can help you make some small changes in your inner space that will empower you as a force for change in your wider world.

I promise we're going to have fun. Despite taking on some heavy topics, *Intention Obsession* is kind of like TikTok—it doesn't take itself too seriously, and neither should you! Get ready to deepen your relationship to pleasure and joy and wonder. Prepare to release self-consciousness, shame, and guilt! We're going to get back in touch with what we loved to do as kids and how magickal we saw the

world before we grew up. We're going to talk to rocks and put our hands in some dirt. We're going to do some things, just to do them! Who cares about results? The journey is the destination.

This book is organized by astrological seasons, so you'll have a little something to do consistently for the whole year. We will be working with the traditional Western archetypes and correspondences of each sign because this is the system that I, as a Westerner and a huge fan of astrology memes, know best. I structured the text this way for a couple of reasons. First, it creates some space between us and traditional interpretations of "time." I think it's important to remind ourselves that many of the ways we organize our lives are made up and can be reimagined. Second, astrology is fun! It's a language that mystics and alchemists and astronomers alike have used for millennia. It works with cosmic systems wholly independent of human meddling. It adds texture and richness to a celebration of the seasons and connects us to our ancestors. They saw shapes in the sky, and thousands of years later we still call the constellations by the names the ancestors chose for them. Even if we can't understand how a clump of stars looks like the scales of justice or a person pouring water from a jug, the collective unconscious has latched on to these symbols for a reason, and that is all we need to know. For now . . .

We'll dive right into Aries season, because astrologically the new year starts in March, with the Spring Equinox. That makes more sense than randomly in the dead of winter, right? (Right.) We'll move through each season with simple practices and rituals for tapping into the specific energies that shape them. The archetypes will lead the way; our job is just to keep showing up.

BEFORE WE BEGIN

BIRTH CHART BASICS

While this book is not a personal astrology book, gathering some information about each sign can help you as you discover the ways in which those archetypal energies are important to you personally. You may know your Sun Sign already, but if not, just start by Googling your birth date and "zodiac sign"! But much more information can be gleaned from diving deeper into your full birth chart, which shows the location of each of the nine planets (Yes, nine! Dwarf planets like Pluto are still important in astrology!) in the solar system on the day you were born and how they interact with one another and the stars. At many sites online, you can plug in your birth date, birth time, and birthplace, and see your whole chart. My personal favorite is astrologer Chani Nicholas's, at https://chart.chaninicholas.com/.

If you're not yet familiar with your birth chart, it's a good idea to look it up and keep a copy nearby as you go through this book. If you start feeling overwhelmed with astral info, I would focus on getting to know your "big three": your Sun Sign, Moon Sign, and Rising Sign. Your Sun and Moon Signs correspond to where the sun and moon were located in the sky when you were born, and your Rising Sign, or Ascendant, as it is sometimes called, is the constellation that was rising on the eastern horizon the moment you were born. You will need your exact birth time to calculate your Rising Sign because it changes every few minutes. By comparison, the sun stays in a particular constellation for an entire month at a time, and the moon for a few days. If you don't know your birth time, or can't access your birth certificate, no biggie! Lots of people don't know their Rising Sign, and they go on to live perfectly normal lives. ☺

Now, I'm no expert in personal astrology. But here's a shorthand I like to use to explain the "big three" placements: your Sun Sign is the story of your life, your Moon Sign is the emotional drama of the story, and the Ascendant, or Rising Sign, is like the book cover. Every astrologer explains the birth chart a little differently, so if you'd like to dive deeper into yours, or astrology basics in general, check the list of my absolute favorite resources in the Further Reading section.

For our purposes here, you really don't need to know anything about your personal chart or astrology at all! Just enjoy the ride!

CORRESPONDENCES

At the beginning of each chapter you will see a list of correspondences for each sign. These associations are informed by centuries of different occult traditions comparing notes and sharing ideas. Some, like the planetary and elemental energy attached to a sign, are more concrete and universally acknowledged. However, some, like the crystal associated with each sign, vary a bit more, depending on the resource you're consulting.

HOW TO "DROP IN"

Now, I'm not really the kind of witch who dons ceremonial robes and treks out deep into the forest to perform everyday rituals like the ones in this book. I do, however, try to create a portal between my everyday life on the material plane and the sacred realm that I want to tap into through my magickal workings by *dropping in.*

Dropping in is like setting the stage for a ritual or spell, and it can look a little different for everyone. The important thing is to feel empowered, connected, and protected. It can be as simple or elaborate as you'd like! I'll let you in on how I like to drop in, and then you can streamline or add on, however you see fit!

We'll start by grounding and centering our energy. Just doing this (steps 1 through 9) can be a powerful way to reconnect to yourself and feel more aligned every day. Whether you feel it or not, as you go through your day, your personal energy gets scattered in a million different directions. To be the most potent and powerful version of yourself, you'll want access to as much of your own energy as possible. So while we can't always control where our energy goes, we can certainly ask for it back. This becomes especially important when connecting with guides and tapping into higher powers.

1. Start by sitting. Take a few deep breaths to come into your body and awareness.
2. Now visualize a green sphere at the base of your spine.
3. Imagine a green cord of energy dropping from that sphere all the way down through your chair, the floor, the ground, the earth's crust, allllllllll the way down to the center of the planet.
4. Give that cord a little tug with your mind. Feel the solid connection between you and the earth. That connection is stable, that connection is healing, and that connection is real.
5. Now take a few more deep breaths.
6. Visualize a white sphere on the crown of your head.
7. Now imagine a white column of light extending from your crown all the way up through the ceiling and the clouds in the sky and out

to the farthest reaches of the cosmos.

8. This is your spiritual connection to the universe, your own guides, and your divine purpose. Let this energy represent the missing ingredient, the invisible, the intangible, the unexplainable.

9. Take a few breaths to feel the green earth energy and the white cosmic energy flowing into your body.

10. Now imagine your own life force energy coming back to you from every direction. You can imagine taking it back from specific places, people, or scenarios, or just keep it vague. I like to visualize this as glittery sparkles coming back into my aura. (An aura is the field of energy that extends about three feet outside your body.)

11. Once you feel grounded and centered in the present moment, you can ask for specific guides you'd like to connect with, ancestors in spirit, or any other divine being you want to invite in to join you!

12. Acknowledge that you are open to receiving wisdom, healing, and support aligned with your authentic purpose and that you are protected from anything that is not aligned with your highest and best outcome.

For me, once I've gone through these steps, I can usually feel the presence of those helpful energies in the form of a warm light around my shoulders and head, and I know that I am "dropped in" and ready to do my tarot spread, cast my spell, or, as in this book, make my snow globe. (You'll see, lol.) You could make it into more of a prayer or song if that format feels more resonant. You might like to dance or move around to feel more connected. As with pretty much anything in this book, follow what resonates with you and leave the rest!

SIGIL BASICS

At a few points in this book I suggest adding a sigil to a project or ritual to help infuse it with intention. A sigil is basically just a magickal symbol created in a specific way to condense a word or statement into a single image. Here's how to make one.

1. Determine your word or statement of intent. Be specific, but try to keep it to a few words or less. For example: Protect my home.
2. Next, rewrite the statement, but take out the vowels and any repeating letters. For example: PRTCMH.
3. Now take the remaining letters, and make a design with them. You can turn the letters in different directions and arrange them in any way you like. You can work on this for a while, drawing it over and over again to make the image as simple as possible. The finished product is your sigil!

A shout-out to my lazy witches (I see you, and I am you): the amazing internet has our back. The website https://www .chaostarot.com/app/ allows you to type in your statement and then creates a sigil for you!

So, are we ready, witches? Gather some jars, look up at the stars, the moon is in Cancer, and the witches say, "The time is right . . ."

Aries Season

Coming in Hot!

March 21–April 19

CORRESPONDENCES

- **SYMBOL:** The Ram
- **DEITY/PLANET:** Mars
- **ELEMENT:** Fire
- **TAROT SUIT:** Wands

- **BODY CONNECTION:** Head
- **CRYSTAL:** Carnelian, or anything red or orange

Strike a match—that's the vibe of Aries season. Aries energy is bold, it's rebellious, it's restless, and it's hot. It's a strong cup of coffee and an unhinged pep talk. It's a young Drew Barrymore standing in front of raging flames with chaos in her eyes (Google "Firestarter 1984"). It's big *Dracarys* energy. But most of all, Aries energy is the perfect antidote to its wintry precursor on the cosmic wheel, the sensitive, dreamy Pisces. Starting things off with a bang, the Spring Equinox hits on the first day the sun moves into Aries, marking the end of winter and the beginning of the season of growth. Represented by the constellation of the Ram, it's hard to imagine a more balls-to-the-walls, up-for-anything, consequences-be-damned energy.

Aries is ruled by the planet Mars. Mars is often seen as *the* god of war in ancient Greek and Roman mythology. But there's something a little more interesting going on with Mars energy, as it actually represents *the enemy*. Armies would call on Venus or Jupiter to aid their side in battle, while Mars represented the opposing force. Therefore, the archetype of Aries carries with it an inherently, shall we say, *oppositional* vibe. But that's totally cool! A little unbridled yang energy, harnessed for good, can be very helpful.

Our first act of rebellion (it won't be our last!) will be against our modern calendar. We'll forge a new path with the power of flame and confront feelings of powerlessness head on!

REBEL AGAINST THE CALENDAR, AS USUAL!

Okay, so why are we starting our year, and this book, in March? Well, why the heck not? Our modern Gregorian calendar was *not* handed down by the universe as some infallible way of keeping track of time. In fact, if any calendar was handed down by the universe, it would probably be the one that our ancestors found in the sky.

Our modern-day version of astrology, and the way it measures time, is the legacy of millennia after millennia of study and worship by just about every culture around the world. From our most ancient prehistoric ancestors in Africa through the Mesopotamians, Greeks, Romans, Arabs, and eventually the early Europeans, astrology has evolved as it has spread all over the globe. Eastern traditions like Chinese astrology and Vedic astrology in India have their own zodiac systems, along with those of the Indigenous American cultures of the Aztec and the Maya, which flourished alongside the system we are working with in this book. Astrology came to humanity instinctively through scientific observation of the natural world, and for most of human history, folks were looking up to the stars to know what was going on down here, on earth.

So then what happened? Well, you may have heard of a certain world-changing and culture-shaping force known as the Christian church.[1] Christian

---

1   You may notice throughout the course of this book that I am heavily critical of the Christian church. It's a dirty job, but someone has to do it. I urge you to understand this critique not as an attack on individual Christian people but a necessary analysis of how the power of the church has oppressed people, colonized the globe, and shaped our Western

leadership saw astrology (and many other scientific and humanistic practices) as competition to their authority and suppressed the practice in Europe for hundreds of years.[2] According to *The Library of Esoterica*:

Considered sacrilege, astrology went underground in the west. As the Roman empire was Christianized, laws were created to punish astrologers, or anyone involved with the practices of magic or divination. . . . Punishments became severe for anyone who acted upon a *curiosita divinandi,* or a "desire to know through divination," and included expulsion and death.

Even before Christianity's rise, the Romans started workshopping the calendar as we know it today. The problem is, like all primeval forces, time itself is wily and cannot be totally contained. The new Julian calendar, established in 46 BCE, broke the year up into 12 months, of roughly 30 to 31 days each, starting on January 1. But they had to account for the fact that the year isn't a perfect 365 days. So they start doing all sorts of tricksy stuff, like leap years and sometimes whole leap *months* to make up the difference. Finally, in 1582 Pope Gregory XIII established the slightly modified Gregorian calendar to better accommodate the actual solar year of 365.2425 days. And that's where we are now.

minds through hierarchy, violence, and the doctrine of shame over the past two thousand years.

2   Outside the domain of the Roman Catholic Church, astrology continued to flourish in other parts of the world. I focus on the branch of Western astrology most directly related to the popular astrology practiced today.

The thing I want you to take away from this is that many of the "truths" we consider timeless and universal definitely aren't timeless or universal. Post-structuralism (something I studied in grad school so you don't have to) teaches us that the foundational structures of our present moment have been intentionally constructed to maintain the power and values of a Eurocentric, patriarchal, Christian supremacy. What we are told is objective truth is actually something constructed to deny our own subjectivity in the interest of control.

All of this to say *it's all made up and we can actually do whatever we want!* Time itself is not linear. History is not linear. Most of the governing systems and structures of the world are just made up by men. Just regular dudes making things up. Which means we, as regular dudes, can also just decide to adhere to our own version of time. Using a different calendar isn't even a radical idea! Plenty of cultural and religious traditions (Jewish, Islamic, Chinese) adhere to their own, while still observing the standard Gregorian.

Personally, I like the zodiac calendar because it speaks to a shared human ancestry and a language that has held meaning outside the hegemonic power structures that have shaped our modern "Western civilization." It also neatly breaks up into twelve seasons, intuitively starting with the season of rebirth that begins on the Spring Equinox. Which to me just makes sense. So by realigning ourselves with a different sense of time, we're also acknowledging that, as Michel Foucault put it in *Power/ Knowledge*, "power is everywhere; not because it embraces everything, but because it comes from everywhere." Maybe even you?

INNER FIRE
CALCINATION SPELL

Okay, who's ready for some spellwork? If you've never cast a spell before, this will be a nice, easy initiation. The important thing is to not be intimidated. A lot of spellwork is simple visualization and concentration. I like to say, "A spell is a prayer with props."

This spell is based on the alchemical process known as calcination. For thousands of years alchemy was a mystical amalgamation of science, magick, psychology, and religion. Unfortunately, in today's popular imagination it's been reduced to old wizards trying to turn common metals into gold (presumably for profit), but the real purpose of alchemy was personal transformation.

The seven-step process that alchemists used to work toward this enlightenment was laid out on a mysterious document carved into a solid piece of emerald, appropriately called *The Emerald Tablet*. No one totally knows where it came from, but the legend and lore (too much to get into here) is super fascinating. Look it up!

Calcination is the first step in the process, and it's the burning away of what is no longer serving you. It's the release of some aspect of your psyche that's holding you back from reaching your full potential. These aspects can be defense mechanisms, limiting beliefs, or just good old-fashioned low self-esteem. Calcination turns these complexes to ash.

While this is a much-simplified version, I hope the knowledge and wisdom of the alchemists of old inspire you to really dig into what you're ready to release as we head into a new season. This easy candle spell will help set an intention for the year to come.

ACCESSORIES

- 1 candle
- 1 piece of paper and something to write with
- 1 fireproof dish
- 1 safety pin
- Matches or a lighter

Remember to "drop in" (page xviii) before starting any spell or ritual in order to connect to a higher power and ask the help of any guides, ancestors, or forces of the universe that are able and willing to assist in creating the highest and best outcome for you and the world around you.

1. Begin by sitting comfortably in front of your candle, paper, and dish. Close your eyes and drop into your body. What does it feel like? What is it holding?

2. Now think of the past few months of your life. What happened during winter that you're ready to release? For me, winter is a time when I welcome stillness and let myself go into "hibernation mode," but come spring, I am ready to move again. Dig deep—the more honest with yourself you can be, the better.

3. Open your eyes, and write a word or two on the paper about what you are ready to let go of. For example: stuck energy, heaviness, scarcity, fear, depression.

4. Say this incantation out loud or in your head:

With this fire,
I clear winter's mire.
Out with cold and
out with the old.
As the past turns to ash,
I can see the light, and
a future so bright.

5. Use the safety pin to carve a word or simple phrase into the candle wax. It should be something counter to what you wrote on the paper. For example: flow, lightness, abundance, bravery, joy.

6. Now light the candle. Observe the flame and how it dances. Behold this primordial force of nature! Fire is so cool and magickal when you really stop to think about it. Take a moment to honor it and offer some gratitude.

7. Carefully use the flame to light a corner of the paper, and place it in your fireproof dish.

8. Watch it burn! As the fire engulfs the paper, imagine the same flame coming from your solar plexus (the middle of your abdomen) and burning away what you want to release. You can close your eyes again if it helps you concentrate, but don't leave your actual fire unattended for too long!

9. Once the paper has fully burned and the fire is extinguished, save a little bit of the ashes. Thank your higher power for aiding you in this magickal work. Next time you're outside, sprinkle the bit of ashes onto some grass or dirt to represent planting seeds for the season ahead.

NOTE: This spell can be repurposed in a million ways! Any time you feel the need to release something, a nice burning spell can really do the trick. You can just modify the incantation or anything else that doesn't fit directly with your intention!

CHARGING AHEAD

Okay, so a big part of witchcraft is charging objects. Basically, you're infusing said object, such as a candle or a crystal, with a specific energy meant to enhance a spell or ritual. While we're riding high on the energetic spark of Aries season, we're going to explore some ways to get creative with charging.

One of the most common practices is charging things with lunar or solar energy. This is done by simply putting the object in a place where beams from the sun or the moon will connect with it. (This method can also be used to energetically clear objects, but we'll get more into that in other seasons.) This easy practice can elevate the power of an object by imbuing it with cosmic, otherworldly energy.

You can also hold something in your hand while meditating on an intention to charge it. Or to attune something to your own positive life-force energy. When I get a new tarot deck or other ritual tool, I like to carry it around with me a bit so it soaks up the vibes of my everyday lived experience. Expanding on that idea, what other meaningful vibes can we harness? You know when people say they wish they could bottle a memory or an experience? It's like that! Here are a few examples of energies I've used to charge objects:

1. The energy of a birthday or another special event
2. The energy of a favorite song
3. Kitty purrs or tail wags from a familiar
4. The energy of a specific place
5. An important astrological transit
6. A favorite color

Recently, I was baking cookies for my coworkers. I tried to be as intentional about adding the energetic ingredients as I was about adding the physical ones. I listened to the song "Break My Soul" by Beyoncé and danced like no one was watching, to bring in the energy of joyful liberation. The moon was full, symbolizing expansion, and I was burning a candle to represent our patron deity Hestia, the goddess of hearth and home, to infuse the cookies with extra warmth and comfort. They came out delicious, and needless to say, everyone at

work was psyched for magickal Beyoncé cookies.

Here's a little fill-in-the-blank to help you get started:

On a night during _____ (insert moon phase, season, or astrological transit) I decided to charge my _____ (object) with the energy of _____ (stated intention). I was aided by the vibrations of _____ (use your senses—what are you seeing, hearing, smelling, tasting, and touching while you charge?) and _____ (an action you are doing to invoke the desired intention). The result will help me honor an intention to _____ (what you will use this object for in your ritual work or everyday life).

SETTING UP AN ALTAR

The cool thing about altars is that, like charged objects, they are the physical representation of the intentions you are setting. You may associate altars with organized religion, but they can be built to honor anything you hold sacred. My wife and I have a love altar on our shared dresser, dedicated to honoring and celebrating our relationship. It holds photos, champagne corks, a copy of our wedding invitation, and other meaningful trinkets from our years together. You probably already have some altars in your home: a family photo wall is an altar to connection. Your carefully curated skin-care shelf is an altar to self-care. Your workspace, with your fancy planner and pretty paperweight, is an altar to channeling your creative force in the material world.

Your altar can also serve as a means of making offerings, such as a simple vessel of water that you change frequently, or something like food, flowers, or even money specifically aimed at honoring a particular deity, ancestor, or spirit guide.

Whether you already have an altar or not, you may want to start a fresh one to correspond with the practices in this book. You can create one on any flat surface such as a fireplace mantel, a shelf on the wall, or even a windowsill, as it does not need to take up a ton of space. It should be in a place that you interact with regularly, to help you stay connected to your intentions. Think of it as a spell that's always being cast.

Your altar should evolve over time. You may want to change out some objects seasonally as you explore this book. As you go through the chapters, some themes and correspondences may resonate more strongly than others. Practice honoring your intuition by finding tangible representations of those symbols. For Aries season, a matchbook, a ram figurine, or anything red or orange would be great options to start with! Set an intention of tending to your altar, even in small ways, every day, to cultivate a devotional practice. You can add to it, take something away, change out any food or water offerings, ring a bell, light a candle, or simply say something nice to it!

GET FIRED UP SPELL: HOW TO HELP WHEN YOU'RE FEELING HELPLESS

Think about the sentence "Make the world a better place." Just saying it may spark an eye roll or a sigh. Thinking about it may feel overwhelming or impossible. You want to make the world a better place, but how can you, one tiny person on a huge planet, actually do so? Well, I've got news for you: each of us holds a unique potential for affecting the world around us. Think about how many times in history a single person has made a huge difference. Rosa Parks simply refused to give up her seat on a bus. She channeled some very Aries traits: boldness, rebelliousness, and most of all bravery.[3]

So, how can you channel your unique traits to create ways of world-changing? We're most effective when we are operating from a place of authenticity and passion. What are you most passionate about? Environmental protections for your community? Animal rights? Affordable housing? Take a little time to meditate on the things that get you fired up. Bonus points if you feel some fire in your body when you think about it. For example, when I think about the fact that billionaires hoard more than half of the wealth of our world while people go hungry and homeless, my heart beats intensely and my arms and legs start to tingle

---

3 Although she is remembered for this single act of incredible bravery, Rosa Parks's activism didn't start there. She served as the secretary for the Montgomery chapter of the NAACP starting in 1943.

with heat. So let's figure out how you can channel your inner ram to "be the change"! After all, activism isn't always about protest signs. Sometimes it's just about Venmo-ing a neighbor in need.

STEP 1: Take a few minutes to ground yourself. You can do this by closing your eyes, taking some deep breaths, and visualizing your body's connection to the earth below. Imagining a green cord extending from the base of your spine to the center of the earth can be helpful.

STEP 2: With your eyes closed, think about the issues that concern you most. Don't go too far into any one thing; just try to see what pops up authentically for you. Maybe there are things close to home? Are there things you're forced to ignore to preserve relationships in your life? Are you bound to a job or career that causes harm? Do you live in an area where the effects of climate change and pollution are affecting people's lives? (Just a few ideas in case global-scale problems feel like a bit much to take on.)

STEP 3: Open your eyes, and write down what comes up.

STEP 4: Look up some ways to help! Use that supercomputer in your pocket to Google what kinds of activism already exist in confronting those issues. Here are a few examples.

- Are you a passionate home chef? Can you bring your skills to help out at a local soup kitchen or food pantry?
- Does someone in your life struggle with addiction or substance abuse? Plenty of folks whose lives have been impacted by addiction have become fierce advocates against prescription drug companies and unfair drug laws and have fought for things like needle exchanges and trauma-informed rehabilitation programs.

- Is poverty an issue in your area? Can you find a mutual aid network to keep you informed of the needs of the community? Direct donations can be much more effective than channeling your money through nonprofits and other organizations.
- You probably like reading, since you're holding this book. Is prison reform or prisoner rights at the top of your list? There are many different angles to approach from, but a simple way we at HausWitch like to engage is through the Prison Book Project. This awesome organization accepts donated books, sorts them to be compliant with the rules of different prisons and jails, and then sends them where they need to go to give incarcerated people the mental stimulation and connection to the outside world that everyone on earth deserves. Fun fact: New Age,

witchcraft, and self-help books are some of the most requested!
- Are you a natural leader who loves to delegate? Maybe you can organize a beach cleanup, clothing swap, or used textile drive.

STEP 5: Keep this list and engage with it whenever you have a little extra time, money, or bandwidth to help make the world a bit better. Or for when you're feeling disempowered in your own life. Sometimes stepping out of ourselves to help others can light a whole new fire in our hearts. Or use this list when you're feeling very powerful! Spread that spark! I dare you!

Okay, witches, don't worry if Aries season made you feel like you burned your candle at both ends. Next we're headed to Taurus season to touch some grass and lie down to relax!

Taurus Season

Luxury and Land

April 20—May 20

- **SYMBOL**: The Bull
- **DEITY/PLANET**: Venus
- **ELEMENT**: Earth
- **TAROT SUIT**: Pentacles

- **BODY CONNECTION**: Neck and shoulders
- **CRYSTAL**: Anything green! Malachite, moldavite, aventurine

Witches! Welcome to Taurus season! Here in the Northern Hemisphere, the spring we were promised a month ago is finally here! The beginning of Taurus season usually falls near Earth Day, when we consider all of the abundance that the earth gives us, and all of the ways that humans can work to restore and repair the harm that colonial capitalism has done to her. That dichotomy is what this chapter is all about. While we exalt ideas like pleasure and rest and sensuality, we also need to stay committed to preserving and defending the actual planet, the literal ground beneath our feet. While climate change is a huge challenge that we will address in further chapters, this season is about the land itself, deepening our connection with it, repairing our relationship to it, and working for the liberation of the descendants of the original inhabitants.

As you can probably tell, my personal feelings toward Taurus season are complicated. On the one hand, it's my favorite time of year; spring is fully sprung and the weather in Salem is finally getting warmer. The flowering trees are blanketing the sidewalks with petal confetti and it just feels better to be alive. On the other hand, people I've known with Taurus placements have embodied the shadow sides of this sign (stubborn, quick to anger, and blunt AF) and made me wary of it altogether. More recently I've welcomed some completely lovely Tauruses into my life, and while they still have those bullish characteristics I mentioned (as we all do), they have taught me about the lighter side of this pleasure-centric earth sign. Taurus is ruled by Venus, after all, the goddess of beauty, love, and fertility. So now, instead of imagining an aggressive raging bull, I picture a happy cow lazing in a meadow, napping in the sunbeams, and that's *definitely* an energy I can get behind.

In this chapter we're going to learn to cultivate sensuality through everyday practices that bring us down to earth, into our bodies, and in touch with our senses. We'll also connect to our local land spirits and learn to channel that Taurus stubbornness into good outcomes! But first . . . we nap.

RADICAL REST RITUAL

This ritual will really help you ground yourself in the magick of Taurus season. You can even order the steps to suit your pleasure! The point is to connect with your softer side by taking a nice long bath or shower, stretching your neck and shoulders to relieve stress, and finally, taking time for rest.

PREPARE: Make sure to wash all the towels, sheets, and clothing you'll be using ahead of time (loose-fitting pajamas or athleisure is the best ritual garb for this and, honestly, every spell). We are going all in, so if you've got nice-smelling laundry soap or dryer sheets, use 'em! Bust out your most luxurious candles and bath and body products. You know, the ones you save for special occasions because they're expensive? Well, this is that special occasion, so light that fancy candle and get ready for Venusian levels of luxury.

BATHE: Be as elaborate as you want here. Bubbles? Yes. Oils? Yes. Shower bombs? Yes. Scrubs, crystals, flowers, herbs, salts? YES! YES! YES! Heck, grab a glass of wine and a snack if you really want to go HAM.

STRETCH NECK AND SHOULDERS: Give yourself anywhere from five to ten minutes to stretch out your neck and shoulders. It's no coincidence that the part of the body ruled by Taurus also happens to hold the most stress and tension. You can find a million stretch tutorials on the internet, but here's a nice, easy go-to if you're trying to stay off your screen. (If you are, you just earned extra credit!)

1. Start by gently bringing your right ear to your right shoulder. After a few breaths, bring your

right hand to your left ear. Don't put too much weight on it, just gently pull. Repeat on the other side.

2. Slowly roll your head back to the right side, bringing your chin through the center. With your right ear back near the shoulder, look down and bring your right hand to the back of your head. Gently pull. Repeat on the other side. Slowly roll your head back through center and look forward.

3. Interlace your hands behind your head, and curl your chin down to your chest. Your elbows will be sticking out in front of you—kind of like bull horns! Hang here for a few breaths.

4. Come back up slowly, and roll your shoulders up and back a few times.

5. Place your hands on your shoulders so that your elbows are sticking straight out to the sides. Rotate your upper body to one side. Flow through the center and twist to the other side. Repeat twice on each side.

6. Reach your hands overhead, and then wrap them around your chest in a giant self-hug. If you want to fold forward from here, have at it! Stay here for a few breaths.

7. Raise your hands overhead one more time, and hug yourself again, but this time with the opposite arm on the bottom. Stay here for a few more breaths.

8. Give your body a gentle wiggle, and let that energy flow!

REST! Now just go to sleep! Power nap (see Capricorn season), or head to bed for the night; it doesn't matter to me. Just so long as you rest. Wrap your clean sheets and blankets around you, and take a few deep breaths to soak in the moment. Blow out any candles before you snooze!

Friday, "Venus Day," is a perfect day to do this ritual, but any time you need to feel a little softness and surrender will work great too!

PLANTING A PLEASURE GARDEN

Planting an herb garden on my porch has been one of the best things I've ever done. Maybe that sounds like an exaggeration, but trust me, the practice of tending to it daily, watching it grow and evolve, and of course harvesting and using my fresh herbs makes me feel in touch with a side of nature that a city kid like me has really never felt. Not to mention that using my fresh-grown herbs to make simple potions gives me big "cottage witch in the forest" nostalgia vibes. I may not have grown up hiking or camping, but your girl definitely made a backyard dandelion stew or two in her day, and it feels nice to get back into that make-believe energy—except this time we can actually use our concoctions! So maybe there's some nice inner-child work for you here too. But before we get ahead of ourselves, I want to reassure you, the main purpose of this ritual is just to give you something good to smell every day.

Some (myself included) might roll their eyes at the very mention of "aromatherapy." The idea has been so co-opted by capitalism that the whole concept seems a little trite. But scent—and its mystical effect on us—is something that fascinated even our most ancient ancestors. Scent is definitely tied to memory, but it can also be a practice in presence. When you are in the act of smelling something, you are situating yourself in the present moment. Learning how to be present is key to cultivating an overall sense of well-being.

Now, black thumbs, I know what you're thinking. I too used to belong to the "I can't do plants" club. Luckily, I'm surrounded by many talented green witches who have helped me become much more adept at keeping plants alive, and I'm here with some easy tips to help you! First off, if you're more of a beginner, use seedlings that have already sprouted rather than starting from scratch with seeds. Here is also where we can channel some of that stubbornness and determination that Taurus is famous for! Do not be discouraged—if your garden dies, plant more seeds (or seedlings). Now is the time, now is the hour. This is the season when you become a plant witch.

PLANT TIPS

- Get a moisture meter. The single most game-changing tool in the plant-care world, IMHO. They cost about ten to fifteen dollars, and all you need to do is stick the sensor end into the soil, and it will tell you if a plant needs to be watered or not. Hard to go wrong.

- Don't want to buy a moisture meter? Use your finger as a moisture meter. Just the tip works fine ☺. Stick your finger into the soil up to your first knuckle. If it feels dry, water the plant. If it feels damp, don't. This technique carried me through my first few years as a plant parent, and it's totally legit. Sometimes though, it is nice to use the moisture meter to see what's going on deeper in the pot, which can't be read with your fingertip.

- Know what's possible with your available sunlight. You may have a backyard that gets full sun all day or a windowsill that gets only a few hours of light a day. One will obviously make it much easier to sustain plant life, but that doesn't mean it's impossible to keep *something* alive in a different setting. Based on my experience as a city witch with no yard and varying levels of natural light, it is important to be very realistic about what's possible since sunlight really makes all the difference with plants.

- Drainage is important! If you are working with a container garden, make sure your pots have holes with drainage dishes, or create a little space at the bottom of the pot with rocks where water can collect separate from the soil.

SMELL IS THE SPELL

When curating your pleasure garden, I want you to really think about which smells light you up. In terms of what we'll be growing outside, I would focus on herbal and/or flower smells. This might take some discovery work on your part. For example, I knew I loved the smell of gardenia and lilac, but until I planted my porch garden, I didn't know that I would find the smell of fresh basil and mint

completely intoxicating. That rubbing a soft little sage leaf between my fingers and then smelling it could spark such joy! But lo and behold, my little experiment in growing fresh herbs to use in fancy cocktails became part of a practice that has completely shifted my life. One of my favorite parts of the day is pouring myself a cup of coffee and watering my herbs in the morning. I talk to them, I sing to them, I tenderly sprinkle a little water on their leaves as well as the soil to send a little bit of the scent wafting into the air. It's delightful!

If you're not one for herbs and want to plant flowers (and you have the space), plant flowers! The important thing is that once a day, you have something fresh and alive to stick your little nose into. If you're not sure which smells you like, go to a nursery and sniff some plants there! Or, more discreetly, you can gently rub a few leaves and then smell your fingers. Once you've figured out the scents you're drawn to, you'll need to assess your space and decide where there's enough light for them to thrive and where your pet friends can't mess with them (I'm looking at my cat, who eats dirt). If you have a backyard, the world is pretty much your oyster. But maybe you have only a windowsill or a tiny porch like mine. That's okay! Use that Taurus determination to figure it out. Even if you have space for only one little pot, give that little guy all you've got.

Either way, the point is to create an easy ritual around tending to your pleasure garden every day. Maybe you come up with a rhyme to say to the plants every morning. Some magick words for your magick herbs. Maybe you just give yourself the five minutes away from your phone that you spend watering and smelling them, and sit in silence. Or maybe you create something more elaborate with moonwater (see Cancer season) and meditations. The basil is in your pot, so go wild.

By the way, if you're still not convinced that this can shift your life just a little bit, talk to any proud plant parent about how good it feels when a new leaf is coming in. You will understand the joy that can be unlocked by tending to plants and herbs.

If you don't think smell is enough to get you out of bed in the morning, here are some magickal correspondences of herbs and flowers that might sweeten the deal.

MAGICKAL PROPERTIES OF HERBS AND FLOWERS

BASIL: This herb gives us courage through trying times and rites of passage and helps break down transition to breakthrough. Basil provides guidance through periods of spiritual growth.

SAGE: Sage can help clear the mind of anxiety and self-limiting thoughts. It creates space for wisdom and common sense to come through. An old adage I like says "Sage, make green the winter rain, charm the demon from my brain."

MINT: There are different types of mint, with peppermint and spearmint among the most common. Either one helps with honoring and embodying divine masculinity and aids in visionary work. (See also mojitos!)

ROSEMARY: Rosemary is a badass. In my head I picture her leaves as magickal barbed wire offering protection from enemies and uncomfortable social situations. Her power isn't just helpful in the material world;

she's also a potent nightmare-buster as well.

THYME: Want to dabble in calling in faeries? Thyme can aid you in conjuring them! They can't help but be lured by the plant's tiny fragrant leaves, and honestly, neither can I! Not ready for a fae party? Thyme can also help you call in purpose and ambition.

OREGANO: Creativity comes from a place of joy and clarity, and oregano is here to assist you in calling that energy in. The scent is bright and clear and wakes up those corners of your mind most in need of a joyful jolt.

LAVENDER: The star of a billion bath-, body-, and bed-related products, lavender is a no-brainer when it comes to dealing with stress. One whiff and you'll know why. Just close your eyes and breathe in stability, awareness, and peace of mind.

LEMON BALM: The leaves of lemon balm smell sweet and bright, perfect for attracting romance! Add this to a self-love bath to increase your attractiveness to others.

GARDENIA: Need a mood boost? Gardenia is the friend whose advice actually helps you feel better by bringing in a sense of peace, healing, and tranquility.

ROSE: I'm sure we're all pretty familiar with this superstar of the plant world. The ultimate symbol of love and beauty, rose calls in heart healing, gaining joy from generosity, and seeing the beauty in all things.

LILAC: Lilac makes a great ghost-buster! But you might be trading one magickal being for another since lilac is also a faerie favorite!

JASMINE: Do you know someone whose confidence seems like a superpower? That's jasmine. She wants to help you with self-confidence and feeling at home in your own energy.

HYACINTH: This flower encourages trust in others while also helping with focus and concentration.

GERANIUM: The geranium helps establish a sense of home and hospitality. It's super easy to care for and it alleviates stress and depression.

FREESIA: Bright and lovely, freesia aids in increasing playfulness and joy and can help relieve grief.

If you planted seedlings rather than grown plants, your garden may not be ready for a harvest during Taurus season. Nonetheless, herbs love to be pruned when needed—it helps them grow! Just be sure to take only a third of the foliage, or less, to keep your little friends happy and healthy.

Here are some creative plant ideas so simple, you can easily experiment and build on what you learn:

EASY HERBAL TISANE: Tisanes are like teas but not. Unlike tea, they are caffeine free and take a little longer to steep. They are literally the easiest thing in the world to make but may still have the power to transport you mentally from city slicker to ancient potion-brewer just the same. All you have to do is put your herbs in a heat-proof container like a teapot, and pour hot, but not boiling, water over them. Let this infuse for about fifteen minutes to an hour or so, and then strain the water into a jar or bottle. My favorite herbs to use for tisanes are mint and lemon verbena. I like to let the tisane cool after steeping and then enjoy it over ice.

PLANT OR FLOWER ESSENCE: Also very easy to make! Place some of your herbs or flowers in a glass bowl when they are at their energetic height. For herbs, this will be once they have grown out a bit from when you planted them and are ready for a pruning. For flowers, this will be when they are at full bloom before they start to fade. Cover the herbs with spring water, and set the bowl in a spot where it will get full sun for at least four hours.

Strain and mix that water with an equal amount of brandy or vegetable glycerin. You can take these essences as medicine for bringing the healing properties of the plant into your physical or energetic body directly or by adding them to drinks, bathwater, or body-care products.

HERBAL OLIVE OIL: You can make herbal-infused olive oils in two ways. One is just by putting an herb in a bottle and covering it with olive oil. Let that sit in a cool, dark place, and in a few weeks, your oil will be infused with all that herbaceous goodness. Just strain and use. Another, faster way is to heat the oil to a simmer, add the herbs, and then let cool. Your herbal-infused oil will be ready to use immediately after straining. My favorite herbs for olive oil are tarragon, rosemary, and thyme. The infused taste may be subtle, so I like to dip fresh bread into it, with a little freshly ground black pepper.

HERBAL ICE CUBES: If you don't cook with fresh herbs very often, it may be hard to coordinate the pruning of your herbs with times when you want to use them in the kitchen. The solution is to preserve your herbs for future use by making ice cubes with them: simply chop them up and place them in ice cube trays. Fill with water and freeze. Then melt the ice cubes when you're ready to use the herbs. You can do the same with flowers to create beautiful ice cubes to use in drinks! (See? I told you there would be pretty ice cubes!)

SIMPLE SYRUP: Simply boil equal parts sugar and water (a cup of each is usually enough) in a pot, and once the sugar is dissolved, add a few sprigs of herbs like rosemary, lavender, or lemon verbena. Cover and let steep for about thirty minutes. Strain the mixture into an airtight container. Use for cocktails and desserts and delicious coffee combos.

DRIED HERBS AND FLOWERS: You can dry your herbs or flowers if you don't want to use them fresh. Hang them upside-down after harvesting but before they start to decay. Simply bundle the sprigs or blossoms, tie them together at the stems, and hang. Once the herbs are crumbly (two to three weeks), remove the leaves from the stems, put 'em in a jar, and use them for cooking. For flowers, create a forever bouquet! This is a really good opportunity to infuse your bouquet with intention before you dry it, or maybe even charge it in some sun or moonlight, and then you will have a beautiful, permanent reminder of that intention. For example, I still have the bouquet my partner sent me on the day I opened the shop. Luckily someone had the sense to preserve it, and now I have the energy of that day with me always. Stay tuned for a Scorpio season ritual that turns that forever bouquet into a spell!

RESEARCH AS RITUAL

Now that we've gotten our hands dirty, it's time to think a little more spiritually. Taurus is an earth sign, but honoring the earth isn't just about digging in the dirt; it's about getting to know the land itself, and its original inhabitants. Doing research on the native plant and animal species that live, or lived, where you do can deepen your connection to the land itself, but also to the ancient energies that predate settler colonial capitalism. Those energies may feel more real to you than the buildings and concrete that surround so many of us. A deep dive may uncover the fact that an animal you have always had an affinity for used to call your city its stomping grounds. Maybe the trees in your neighborhood have been there for hundreds of years. There are sycamore trees in Massachusetts that predate the so-called United States altogether. I bet that's the case in your area as well! But don't stop at living things! What kind of soil and rocks are abundant near you? What are the bodies of water? Research will help foster a connection to these entities and add oomph to your magickal practices, but it will also situate you within the wider web of nature and all the forces it embodies.

OFFERING TREE

I can think of no more powerful symbol of grounding than the roots of a tree. Not only do the roots hold the tree securely in place, often for hundreds of years, but they carry messages underground to other trees and beings in the soil. Stability *and* wisdom? YES, PLEASE! In this practice you'll get to know a tree in your neighborhood and give it some love and attention whenever you have the chance.

Start by finding a tree you're drawn to and researching

what it is. You can use a good old-fashioned field guide or a plant-ID app.

Try to establish a psychic connection with the tree. You might just gently place a hand on its bark or leaves. You can introduce yourself (speaking in your head or out loud), and just let the tree know how much you admire and respect it.

Don't take anything off the tree without asking first. Resist the urge to take; the point here is to give.

Now bring it offerings whenever you feel compelled! An offering can be words of affirmation, a cool rock, a little song, a wave, a secret, a flower, or even a kiss! As a person with access to an abundance of crystals and tumbled stones, I love to leave a sparkly treasure in the soil at the base of a tree I feel connected to.

LAND BACK

By now, we all know about the genocide and land theft that European settlers inflicted on the First Nations people

of the Americas, Africa, the Caribbean and Pacific Islands, and Australia. The devastation of such imperialism has never been properly acknowledged and can never be fully repaired. As a white person who has benefited greatly from that dynamic, I find it easy to be overcome by shame and resistance when confronted by the legacy of settler colonialism and how it is still benefiting me to this day. No matter how you slice it, a great many of us hold the positions we have because of the land and resources stolen from the Indigenous groups who lived here first. This can be paralyzing, but in order to transmute that feeling of helplessness, we have to push through it. How can we bear witness, which is a bare-minimum reparative act? What else can we do in the present to honor and exalt the descendants of those folks in the present day? Here are some ideas.

Start by familiarizing yourself with the tribes who inhabited the land where you live before colonization. There is an amazing tool for this online at https://native-land.ca. Here you can put in the city or town where you live and find out which groups originally inhabited its land. Here in Salem, Massachusetts, the Naumkeag band of the Massachusett tribe used this land as their summer hunting and fishing grounds before European colonizers displaced them.

A little farther south, around the area of Plymouth, a band called the Wampanoag were stewards of the land and still live in the area. Organizations like the Wôpanâak Language Reclamation Project strive to reconstruct the original languages of the Massachusett tribes in an effort to preserve their culture. It has been not only an honor to support the

WLRP both monetarily and by hosting informational sessions at HausWitch, but also a fascinating experience in seeing how cultural hegemony works on a practical level. European Christian colonizers did not "win" this land because they were destined to or because they were more righteous and deserving than the First Nations peoples. It is instead because the colonizers systematically and violently attacked them, and also used equally sinister yet more insidious means to suppress them, such as banning their languages, culture, and religious rights.[1]

It is time to stand in solidarity with Indigenous peoples. We can't right all of the collective wrongs imposed upon Native Americans, but we can make an effort to be in right relationship with their descendants.

---

1 Here's a good example. Many folks have adopted the Indigenous practice of burning white sage as a way of clearing their home of negative spirits. But in the United States, Native Americans themselves were banned from performing this practice until 1978, when the American Indian Religious Freedom Act was passed. In addition to other ethical issues surrounding white sage (such as the overharvesting of the plant to keep up with

In recent years, Indigenous activism has gained some real ground all around the world. Territory is being recognized and returned in places like Panama, Peru, Cambodia, Australia, and even the United States. In June 2021, the Keystone Pipeline project was officially canceled after more than a decade of Native-led protests. The project would've been disastrous for sacred Indigenous land and religious sites and also for the freshwater aquifer that runs through the land. In many cases, Indigenous rights are inextricably linked to environmental rights, stressing the need to create a sustainable existence in harmony with nature.

The most important thing is to familiarize yourself with the ways in which Indigenous groups are directly asking for support. If you can't find any organizations local to you, perhaps you could support the wider #landback movement, which aims to restore Indigenous political and economic authority over the land they occupied historically. In 2020 the movement began working toward reclaiming the Black Hills area around Mount Rushmore, known to the Sioux as the Six Grandfathers. You can read their manifesto at https://landback.org.

All right, my beautiful bulls, I hope that Taurus season has been a portal of rest and reconnection for you. Cherish that grounded feeling now, because next we're heading into the ethereal whirlwind that is Gemini season!

---

rampant consumption and the argument that burning white sage in particular by non-Indigenous folks is culturally appropriative), this aspect especially speaks to the kinds of tactics settler colonialism has used to decimate any sense of sovereignty that the Indigenous peoples of the "united states" previously held. Fucked up, right? In some ways though, the tide is finally turning. In 2020 the United Nations declared 2022–32 as the Decade of Indigenous Languages: "It will prioritize the empowerment of Indigenous language users and place Indigenous Peoples at the center of all planning, as based on the foundational principle of 'nothing for us without us.'"

Gemini Season

Start the Conversation

May 21–June 20

- **SYMBOL:** The Twins
- **DEITY/PLANET:** Mercury
- **ELEMENT:** Air
- **TAROT SUIT:** Swords

- **BODY CONNECTION:** Hands and lungs
- **CRYSTAL:** Fluorite

Hello, hello! Welcome to easy, breezy Gemini season! Well, easy for me because, full disclosure, I am a proud Gemini Sun and Mercury! What feels light and effortless for me has been known to feel wild and chaotic for some . . . but in the best way! Coming at a time when spring is transitioning to summer and the air just feels *alive*, what's not to love?

As Chani Nicholas puts it in her book *You Were Born for This*: "Not exactly loyal to any one idea, Gemini roams around as many thoughts as it possibly can to get a better grasp of a subject. . . . Like winds blowing in different directions, you can appear to be everywhere and nowhere at once. . . . Inward and outward, reflexive and responsive, introverted and extroverted, Gemini contains contradictions."

If you ever struggled to pick between two entrées at a restaurant, desperately wishing you could order a half portion of both, or if you're always the one playing "devil's advocate," or if, like me, talking is your drug of choice, you're already familiar with Gemini energy. It's two for the price of one! Opposites attract! Communication! Information! Stimulation! We contain multitudes!

Confused? So am I! But that's precisely Gemini's zone of excellence. Sorting through uncertainty and holding space for both sides comes as second nature to Geminis. Just don't ask us to make a choice. If we can't merge the opposites, we're a little lost. But even being lost is a more comfortable place for Gemini than most. As Linda Goodman writes in *Love Signs*, "To Gemini, truth is a great rolling ocean, rainbow hued and glittering, filled with the fish of many-faceted half-truths, maybes, ifs and possiblys."

In classical mythology Gemini is represented by the twins Castor and Pollux. Half-brothers, one mortal and one immortal, these two loved each other so much that they refused to spend the afterlife apart, in heaven or on earth. Zeus's solution was to put them in the sky together for eternity, symbolizing the dual nature that we all have inside us.

The eternal conversation between Castor and Pollux is only *part* of why Gemini is considered the chatterbox of the zodiac. This season is ruled by Mercury, "messenger of the gods," who held the special privilege of bouncing between all three realms (heaven, earth, and the underworld) to carry correspondence from Olympus. Mercury is also known as a trickster, an eternal child, and a shape-shifter. Honestly, this guy would do anything to get the message across, and so will we.

So how can we honor and embody this dynamic archetype? Through its most well-known and dominant trait, communication.

GREET YOUR GUIDES!

We all have spirit guides, and whether you have communicated with them directly or not, they have communicated with you. Guides connect with you through your intuition, dreams, synchronicities, divination, and visions—to name just a few possibilities. There are also different types of guides, who will connect with you in their own specific way. Guides can be ancestors, angels, animals, loved ones who have passed away, or any other spiritual entity who provides psychic support. You may already be well acquainted with some or all of your guides. You may have never thought about them (consciously) a day in your life. Either way, this exercise will help you connect to an unseen force that has your back, maybe in unexpected ways.[1]

If you've never felt the presence of a guide or are feeling a little lost, I highly suggest my favorite book on the subject, *The Seven Types of Spirit Guide* by Yamile Yemoonyah. She does an amazing job of explaining the whole concept of spirit guides and even provides a fun quiz for identifying who some of your guides may be (doing outside research is another way to align with information-obsessed Gemini energy)![2]

For example, I feel a strong connection to the energy of

---

1   As with all spells, you can elaborate on these ideas endlessly. There are many good sources with information about building out rituals and connecting with helpful spirits. My goal is simply to help you find ways to connect to these forces easily in your everyday life. Geminis LOVE information. But if it feels too "quick and dirty" for you to plunge right in, I invite you to check out the Further Reading section for some of my favorite magickal research materials.

2   There is a free online version of the quiz here: https://yemoonyah.com/quiz/.

my close loved ones who have
passed on and connect with
them through little signs that
I understand consciously. For
example, my dad often lets me
know he's around through music.
A shared favorite song, like
"Don't Change" by INXS, will
come on at just the right moment
to help me feel his presence
when I need it.

My animal guides, cats, are
supportive in less obvious
ways. From the white tiger

that my grandmother took me
to see at the zoo when I was
a baby, to the black panther
that I see in meditation
stalking in a protective circle
around me, to the Egyptian
goddess Bastet who shows up
when I receive energy work,
big feline energy is always
making itself known in my life.
Most important, it has given
me good instincts that have
led me to safety and protection
throughout my life.

Possibly the biggest "sliding door" moment in my life came when I was fourteen years old. My parents had been on the verge of splitting up for years, and one day I came home from school to find my mother had finally decided to leave. Despite her suffering from mental illness for my whole life, my mom and I were *super* close. Some might even say enmeshed (yes, I would say enmeshed). We had even talked about what would happen if my parents split up. Her plan was this: I would stay with my mom, and my sister would stay with my dad. But when push came to shove, and she called to say she was coming to get me, I told her I wanted to stay right where I was, living with my dad.

I could never fully explain that decision through logic, but it actually saved my life. It has always felt like divine intervention, but it wasn't until I was discussing this with a therapist, who called out my on-point instincts, that I put the pieces together. As anyone with a housecat knows, cats have amazing instincts and are the world's leading experts on finding comfort, safety, and protection. The way my animal guides showed up for me that day helped override the way I had been conditioned to favor my mother, so I made the decision that supported my survival. Despite our closeness, my mother was not the safest protector for me in that situation, while my dad was able to provide a stable, supportive environment. To say I will always be grateful to my feline guides for nudging me in the right direction is an understatement.

So as you can see, guidance can come in many forms, conscious or unconscious. To get started, let's simply let your guides know that you would like to connect.[3]

---

3   There are many guided meditations on the internet and a full ceremony in *The Seven Types of Spirit Guide* if this one doesn't work for you.

1. Start by making yourself as comfortable and relaxed as possible. If you have any rituals or routines around relaxing, now is the time to practice them. (The Taurus season Radical Rest Ritual will work!)

2. Set the intention to connect with your guides, while not asking for anything in return (for now). If you regularly work with divinatory tools like tarot, runes, or journaling, you may want to have them close by, but they are not a must.

3. Do a quick check-in about what you need to set the mood. Just close your eyes for a minute and see if any ideas pop into your head. Maybe you have a prayer candle, figurine, or crystal that wants to sit in.

4. Once you're comfortable, close your eyes, take three deep breaths, and ground yourself.

5. Now, whether you know who they are or not, gently ask for only the most supportive energies to come through, to align with the highest and best outcome for you and all beings on earth.

6. Once you feel a connection, think about what to say. This can be as simple as introducing yourself (you can pretend they don't already know everything about you) or as elaborate as you want. If you have performance anxiety, you may want to jot down a few notes or a script beforehand (but, though it's Gemini season, don't overcomplicate this process, which is just a chance to say hi). I might say something like "I know you are always with me, but I am connecting intentionally to let you know that I am so grateful for your support and am open

to receiving communication from you."

7. Spend a few minutes in that energy.

8. That's it! You may receive some feedback, and you may not. Even if you don't feel any signs of having made contact, you have.

9. Alternatively, your guides may come through with messages or requests for other ways of connecting. You may feel called to honor them with a physical representation of them on your altar. You may have a prophetic dream or be able to pick up on messages through one of your senses. No matter what, if you get a message, honor it!

P.S. So, a funny and really cool thing happened the day after I wrote this ritual—a "new" guide greeted ME! A powerful witch friend was leading a workshop at my shop when a purple-hued energy made itself known as a personal guide of mine, who had come to earth to help me with my work here! When my witch friend told me about it later, I immediately burst into happy tears because I could feel that it was true on a deep level. Although we had never been formally introduced, *Purple*, as I now refer to them, has been a nurturing presence I have felt strongly throughout my life, and I'm grateful to be able to connect more intentionally now!

So you just never know who's on your etheric A-team! Even an experienced witch like me is still meeting new guides all the time, and just because I didn't know about them consciously before doesn't mean they haven't been with me all along.

"JUST THE MESSENGER" AUTOMATIC WRITING SPELL

Now that we've consciously connected to our guides, let's see what they might have to say. In a slightly counterintuitive move for Gemini season, this time we're mostly going to listen. Try this out on a Wednesday, Mercury's fave day.

Automatic writing provides the most crystal-clear form of spirit communication I can imagine. It's also exactly what it sounds like: asking for messages and then writing down what comes into your mind automatically. The most important thing to remember is that you are "just the messenger," the vessel through which Spirit is trying to communicate. Your big ol' brain can just switch itself right off. An empty head is honestly the best tool here. Your only job is to be as clear and open as possible.

One part of the body that Gemini corresponds to is the hands, so we're going to be channeling our guides' messages through them. You can use paper and pen, or a computer. Even your notes app will work, although based on the borderline-toxic relationship I have with my phone, I would caution against digital divination!

ACCESSORIES
- Pen
- Paper

1. Start with the Greet Your Guides! meditation.
2. Once you've made contact or at least made your intention known, imagine a clear or white column of light coming down from the cosmos through the crown of your head, down the center of your body, and out through your hands.

3. With your eyes closed, rub your hands together until you can feel them generate some heat. Then pull them about six inches apart, and see if you can feel the energy going back and forth from one hand to the other.

4. Now pick up your pen and be patient.

5. Write whatever comes to mind. Don't edit yourself! The line between your "imagination" and the way your guides connect can be extremely blurry! Whatever comes through, go with it!

6. Try switching to your nondominant hand. Messages may be more likely to come through mental pathways other than those you use in your everyday life.

7. If nothing comes through naturally, ask for just one word. That will come through. Write it down, no matter how silly or strange it seems. Gemini is the season of the silly and the strange!

8. Over the next few hours, days, or weeks, see how that word or message shows up in your life.

9. If you'd like to cultivate this practice, maybe start by asking for one word a day for a week. Ask for guidance about what would be helpful for you to consider on that day. Sort of like a one-card tarot pull.

10. Once you feel comfortable, why not start a convo with your "twin"—your higher self, your unconscious! Try to intentionally connect. You can work with dreams, synchronicities, or signs and symbols that come up frequently. For example, ask for more information about a dream or an uncanny coincidence that happened the other day. What are they trying to teach you? Or why do ladybugs keep appearing at significant moments?

11. If you are a writer, this spell can be a great way to connect with your muses! I would say that most of the writing in this book is channeled!

ANIMISM AND COMMUNICATING WITH HOUSE SPIRITS

Have you ever heard the phrase "If these walls could talk"? Well, guess what? THEY CAN! So can your pots and pans! And your bathtub! Since you're reading this book, you probably already talk to your pets and plants. Maybe you even catch yourself talking to other so-called inanimate objects already; if you don't, now's the time to start. If connecting with spirit guides didn't come naturally to you, our next conversation might just feel like second nature. It's time to reconnect with our most primal way of relating to the world: animism.

For most of human history, animism was inextricably tied to the way humans moved through the world. At its most basic, animism is the belief that everything, and I mean everything, has its own distinct life-force energy. To an animist, plants, animals, objects, grass, furniture, storms, mountains, molehills, and everything in between have a spiritual essence. This way of relating to the world kept humans aligned with their

environment and respectful of natural resources. Nonhuman beings were thought of as family, part of one's community, and they were treated as such. Can you imagine if we acted with this much care for the world around us today? In an absolutely incredible episode of his podcast *The Emerald*, titled "Animism Is Normative Consciousness," Josh Schrei explains:

Only in the last 500 years, a tiny sliver, one tenth of 1 percent of human history, do we find in the Western world what we call the post-animate era. . . . Animism is normative in the sense that so deeply is it ingrained into the human heart, and mind, and eye, so deeply inherent is animism that there wasn't even a word for it until the 1800s. It was never described as anything other than simply the way things are. The water in which we swim.

Because animism is completely incompatible with the project of colonial capitalism, we have largely lost touch with it. Looking at the world through the lens of modern life, we can see why we have to reject the idea that everything is alive in order to uphold the way our contemporary world functions. A key component of capitalism is viewing everything as a resource toward generating profit, and any consideration of unique life-force energy is secondary or nonexistent. It's the difference between trees and logs. Trees grow in intentional ways, and it has been proven that they have friendships and can communicate with one another and with us. But are those things considered before a forest is clear-cut for industry? Of course not, because those trees aren't seen as sentient beings; they're seen as logs.

But for a lot of us, that doesn't feel right. I believe we come into the world relating to animism as 98 percent of our ancestors did, and despite Western society's discouraging messaging, I believe part of us stays that way. This may explain why as children we feel so comfortable talking to toys and trees and teddy bears.

An example I like to use is Wilson from the movie *Castaway* (spoilers ahead!). In the film, Tom Hanks's character, Chuck, is stranded, completely alone on a deserted island with only the contents of a few packages that wash up on shore to help him survive. One of the boxes contains a volleyball. In a moment of frustration over an injury to his hand, Chuck throws the volleyball, leaving a bloody handprint. The handprint sort of looks like a head, so he draws a face. He names his new friend Wilson, after the manufacturer. He begins talking to Wilson, who has his own personality, and he responds to Chuck in conversation. Not out loud, but

Chuck knows how to listen. Their relationship provides moments of comic relief and shows how important connection is, even in the most dire survival situations. In the context of the film, all of this works because we can relate. Even if we don't talk to our stuff now, something inside us can remember a time when we did. Arguably one of the film's most emotional moments comes when Chuck loses Wilson, in a genius cinematic moment that lands only because of the audience's innate connection to animism.

Whether I have you convinced about animism or not, we're gonna start a conversation with your house. Establishing a deeper, familial relationship to your home is a great way to start reprioritizing the animate and feeling more connected to your home space. This can be a great way of connecting to your inner child, and Gemini season is the perfect time for that too.

AT HOME WITH YOUR HOUSE SPIRITS!

Many cultures across time and space have formed relationships with house spirits. Let's start with a few questions to find where your deepest natural connection to your home lies, and then we'll get a little chatty.

WHAT ARE THE MOST IMPORTANT WAYS YOUR HOUSE SUPPORTS YOU? Is your kitchen the beating heart of your home because cooking is your love language? Is nourishment the most important thing your home provides? Or is it rest? Or privacy?

IF YOUR HOME WERE A PERSON, HOW WOULD YOU DESCRIBE THEM? Get creative! I think my home would be a nineties kid. When my wife and I first moved in, all we wanted to do was blast nineties music and watch movies from that time. I think my home was an "it girl" who's aging pretty gracefully. She loves to keep her styling classic but can't help

being into all the latest trends. She's the friend who remembers everyone's birthday and is always down to host a dinner party or a porch hang.

HOW CAN YOU CONNECT WITH THE SPIRITS OF THINGS? Gratitude is one way, but what are some others? I like to name things. My cat is my best friend, but I spend A LOT of time with my couches, Soft Island and Cozy Cove, so could they not be seen as supportive friends too? I named my huge Dutch oven Lois after my grandmother because she carries the sturdy, strong energy it takes to cook up a big batch of delicious stew. Not all of our thirty-plus plants

have names, but a lot of them do! Don't even get me started about my shop. Everything from the sales counter to the crystals have names, and it's a pretty enchanting place to be, if I do say so myself!

HOW CAN YOU BECOME A MORE "CONSCIOUS COLLECTOR"?

When we acknowledge the energy and aliveness of our "possessions," we honor the meaning they represent in our lives. The main reasons we bring things into our homes have to do with form, function, and feeling. Some things are utilitarian, some are just beautiful. But the artifacts of life, such as photos, souvenirs, collectibles, heirlooms, and gifts, carry their own kind of magick. Souvenirs are portals to other places. Heirlooms are portals to ancestors. Photos are time machines! What magickal

properties do your house friends carry?

WHAT CONVERSATIONS ARE ALREADY HAPPENING IN YOUR HOME? How can you

add intention into your space by creating conversations between your things? Would that souvenir from your trip to the tropics like to be closer to your tropical plant? Maybe the seashell you brought home from the beach wants to be on a windowsill so she can still see the sun. Can you display that necklace from your grandmother on an altar rather than hiding it away in a closet?

Okay, so I know that was A LOT, but once you've had a chance to think about these questions, you're ready to talk to your house!

"EVERYTHING IS ALIVE" SPELL!

1. When you wake up in the morning, before you get out of bed, set the intention to view everything in your home as *alive*.

2. Greet everything you interact with. "Good morning, toothbrush! How are you today?" Listen for an answer, but it's totally okay if you don't "hear" anything at first. Remember all the psychic skills you picked up earlier in this chapter! You may get a verbal answer, or you may get . . . something else . . .

3. Check in with your collections and vignettes. Do they like being arranged together? Does anyone want to move?

4. If it helps, you can use Post-it notes or googly-eye stickers to create faces on things. Just get weird! It's fine! And fun!

5. Try to make a connection with as many things in your space as you can. Thank them for being friends.

6. Is there anything you don't feel a positive connection to? Maybe there are some relationships that aren't a good fit.

7. Close by saying good night to everyone.

Is all of this feeling a little *too* silly? Just start small! Say hello and goodbye to your space every day. I bet you'll start to notice a difference in how the space feels!

Okay, now that you've formed magickal relationships with your spirit guides, your toaster, and your space, it's time for one last chat . . .

LET'S HAVE A "CONGRESSIONAL KIKI"

By now we know that posting things on social media and showing up to vote every few years is not enough to bring about freedom and justice for all. Democracy requires participation, and whether our elected officials want to admit it or not, the more participation the better. Especially from intentionally marginalized communities. While the idea of government and politics doesn't conjure up the sexiest vibes, reaching out to your reps doesn't have to be stressful or boring! Let's make it a kiki!

What's a kiki? The term, like so much else in contemporary pop culture, comes from the Black LGBTQIA+ community and was popularized through drag culture. It entered mainstream culture in 2010 with the Scissor Sisters' song "Let's Have a Kiki." Put simply, it's a gathering of friends . . . for the purposes of chatting and gossiping. What could be more Gemini than that?

I'll tell you what—a tangent! While we're here, let's have a kiki about queer history in honor of Gemini season overlapping with Gay Pride Month!

A PROTEST AND A PARTY

June is celebrated as Gay Pride Month in honor of the Stonewall Riots of 1969. In brief, Stonewall was a queer-friendly bar that catered to all echelons of queer society, especially the working class, people of color, and trans and gender-nonconforming folks. Because of this, it attracted a certain brand of revolutionary. Since it was harder for these people to remain closeted and live within a heteronormative paradigm, they were inevitably less attached to the idea of flying under the radar and fitting in. The bravery it took for these folks to live their truth lent itself to the IDGAF energy that culminated in the "riots." After decades of police raids and harassment, on June 28, 1969, the folks at Stonewall decided to fight back. When the police got violent with one of the bar's lesbian patrons, the crowd began throwing anything they could get their hands on at the police. They barricaded the officers in the bar and held their ground on the streets outside. The protest lasted for five days and involved thousands of people. Queer life in America would never be the same, and the next year, 1970, the Gay Liberation Front put on the first Gay Pride March on June 28, in honor of Stonewall.

While the queer liberation movement definitely picked up steam in the 1970s because of Stonewall, queer people have always existed, and so has their fight for acceptance. So much of what popular culture equates with LGBTQIA+ culture comes from the masquerade balls of the Harlem Renaissance. Modern drag culture had a rich history throughout the twentieth century in New York's Black communities. If you think Madonna invented voguing, now is the time to watch the documentary *Paris Is Burning*.

Intention Obsession

At a time when Gay Pride Parades have become partially co-opted by corporations and "rainbow-washing," we can still enjoy the partylike atmosphere of Pride as an important entry point for society to engage with the queer community. However, while in some parts of the world LGBTQIA+ folks are enjoying expanded acceptance and freedom, religious zealots are working harder than ever to destroy those gains. Currently, as I write this, there are FIVE HUNDRED anti-trans bills going through the US legislative process, in forty-nine out of fifty states. This form of violent "othering" is nothing new for the gay community, and it carries all the markers of a modern-day witch hunt. The idea of gay pride may be more popular than ever, but it's important to keep in mind that queer folks are still literally fighting for their lives and liberation every single day.

So let's join in the fight! Whether you feel passionately about big-picture issues or ones that are closer to home, it's time to get to know your elected officials so you know who to call when it's time to hold our government accountable.

Start by getting to know who the heck these people are. Sure, we all know who the president is, but do you know your senators and representatives? What about even closer to home? You might know your mayor, but what about the city council? The school board? These are literally the people whose job it is to act in our best interest, and I don't think they hear from us enough!

What are they all about? How do they vote on issues? If they always vote in a way that conflicts with your values, it's time to tell them that! That's what Gemini season is all about!

Next, gather their contact info. Or at least know where to find it online. If you're still a little lost,

the website https://5calls.org is a great place to start. You can enter your location and the issues that are important to you, and it will tell you exactly who to have a kiki with, or alternatively, read for filth.

Contacting your reps and senators is easy as pie. Have anxiety? Call after the offices are closed and leave a message. Write a sassy script for yourself. Channel your inner drag queen, and just say what you mean, honey! If you don't have any problem speaking with people on the phone, you can learn more from the office staff by calling during the day and asking about whatever issue you're dealing with.

Create a character or a persona if you need to. Maybe you have trouble asserting yourself. In the spirit of Gemini season, can you create an alter ego who doesn't?

Emailing is super easy—you can even write one and just keep sending it every day! But make it a good one. Get creative! Maybe it starts with "First of all, how dare you?"

Our democracy is literally hinging on this form of communication. Elections are only one piece of the puzzle. Once we elect our officials, they need to know what we support or reject, and it's up to us to tell them! So don't just stand there, let's get to it—call your reps, there's nothing to it!

Okay, my little Gems, if you're feeling a little dizzy, that's all right! It's time to dive into the calming waters of Cancer season!

Cancer Season

Deep Dive

June 21–July 22

- **SYMBOL:** The Crab
- **DEITY/PLANET:** The Moon
- **ELEMENT:** Water
- **TAROT SUIT:** Cups
- **BODY CONNECTION:** Chest, breasts, and stomach
- **CRYSTAL:** Moonstone, rose quartz

Are we ready to *go with the flow*? Good, because Cancer season is nothing if not an invitation to surrender. She's crashing waves and rolling tides. She's seashells in the sun, and the cool, dark depths of the sea. Like the motion of the ocean, Cancer season either happens *with* you or *to* you. You can bottle it up, or cry it out. I suggest the latter.

People with Cancer placements see emotional release as a sport. Don't let this water sign fool you; we're not here to sit still in a pool of our own tears. We are MOVING. We are feeling our feelings. Stuck energy is the enemy. Even if it looks messy on the outside, the Cancer trait of navigating deep emotionality is its superpower.

Cancer, symbolized by the crab, is all about hard, protective shells and soft, vulnerable middles. The home space is especially important to Cancer energy, both in the need to feel held and nurtured and the need to hold and nurture others.

Cancer is ruled by the moon rather than a planet. Traditionally gendered feminine, the moon represents cycles, fertility, and the subconscious. Like most things relegated to the realm of the divine feminine, she has been depicted as playing second fiddle to the sun for over a thousand years. But that wasn't always the case. You only have to consider the length of our months (moonths) to understand how integral it has been for humans to align with the moon.

So while society at large may devote itself to the sun, we as witches love to worship the moon. Especially during Cancer season. So this moonth we're going to start with some basic lunar magick, and then crab-walk ourselves onto the beach to work with the primordial forces of water and salt.

"JUST A PHASE" MOON SPELLS

Every lunar cycle has five main phases. The new moon appears in the sky after three days of darkness. It's the tiny silver sliver that starts the cycle over again. The moon's transformation from a crescent to a half moon and eventually a full moon is known as the waxing phase. The peak point is the full moon. This is as big, bright, and round as she gets. After that her appearance starts to decrease, and this is called the waning moon. Finally, the last part of the cycle is the dark moon, when it appears as though the moon has disappeared entirely.

Each phase corresponds with a specific type of spell work, and for me personally, observing the phases of the moon is foundational to the kind of magick I practice. Here's a quick rundown of the types of rituals that work well with each phase, some simple spell ideas, and quick incantations too.

THE NEW MOON

The new moon is the best phase to start. Start what? Anything.

A new habit, a new project, a new adventure. It's a time to plant seeds, literal or otherwise.

"TRY SOMETHING NEW" MOON SPELL: You may already have an idea for seeds you want to plant during the new moon, but if you don't, trying something new is a great way to open up your world, even in tiny ways. Let the moon inspire you to try a food you've never had, or an outfit you've never worn. Take a new route to work, or start a class in something you've always been interested in.

> Trying something new,
> Revealing something true;
> Aligning with the moon
> To sing a different tune.

THE WAXING MOON

When the moon starts to appear bigger in the sky, *we* should also be focusing on amplifying and expanding. This is the time for manifesting spells, or anything else that grows or attracts.

"WAXING POETIC" MOON SPELL: Write your own glow-up. Take a little time to think about what you want to amplify in your life. Think about nice things you want to say to or about yourself! Be outrageous! Now write it down as if it's already true. Now is the time to let your goals and desires take up some serious space in your life.

For example, something I could write at this moment might be "Writer Erica Feldmann tops the bestseller list with *Intention Obsession*, a masterfully written book that everyone needs. Feldmann took immense care to create an offering that is accessible to anyone and interesting to everyone."

> Let these words ring true,
> See this future through.
> As the moon grows,
> My intention flows.

THE FULL MOON

The full moon is about celebration and illumination. Use it to shine a light on something you manifested or grew during the waxing phase or to celebrate something that helps you feel empowered or aligned.

"FULL MOON, FULL HEART" SPELL: One of my favorite sayings is "Gratitude is heaven itself." Because it's true! For me, any time I'm feeling some type of way, I always reach for gratitude. No matter what, you can always find something to feel grateful for, even if it's just the air in your lungs. During the full moon, find something you feel grateful for and make an offering to the moon to say thank you to the universe. This could be anything from lighting a candle to something more elaborate. The only must-have tools are intention and gratitude.

Full moon bright,
Lighting up the night,
Thank you for the light.
Everything feels right.

THE WANING MOON

After the full moon, we go through the waning phase. As the moon appears smaller in the sky, we want to look for things in our lives that should decrease. Things that are obstacles to our goals and aspirations. Now is the time to let go.

"WANING AND DRAINING" SPELL: Think of something that's draining you: something like a bad habit, contact with a toxic person, or just negative self-talk. Now take a glass or bowl of water and whisper the details to it. Tell it all about what you're trying to release and why. Hold the vessel in your hands for a few minutes while you close your eyes and visualize the moon getting smaller and smaller, from a half moon all the way back to a tiny crescent. Then simply whisper "Goodbye" to the water and pour it down the nearest drain or flush it down the toilet.

Then, repeat these words:

THE DARK MOON

The dark moon phase is the perfect time for clearing. The moon has fully waned and again appears as a tiny crescent, eventually becoming invisible to the eye.

"DARK MOON DINNER" SPELL:

This spell is super practical and I love it. Make a meal out of stuff that's about to go bad in your fridge. One time my wife and I wanted to make dumplings, but we had only a few of the ingredients we needed. But we also had some greens that were about to perish, some sauces and condiments that were on their last legs, and so on. It happened

to be the dark moon, so we let that inspire us to make "dark moon dumplings," so nothing would go to waste. They were delicious! But you don't have to stick to dumplings—make yourself a feast of whatever cuisine you're craving.

Dark moon clearing,
Light disappearing,
New from old, a little treat.
The perfect time to make
and eat!

WATER WORKS

Making moonwater is a great way to dip your toes into lunar magick. Start by finding a special vessel, preferably made of glass or ceramic. Fill it with filtered or spring water, and put it in a place where the moon will shine on it. Depending on what you're planning to use it for, you may want to cover it so that nothing falls in while it's charging. Spend a few minutes holding the bowl and connecting to an intention (even if that intention is just "making moonwater"). That's it! Store your moonwater in a jar or bottle, and keep it on hand for future magickal workings!

As you can see, making moonwater is pretty straightforward, but there are a few ways to add some extra intention.

- Take into account the phase and astrological sign the moon is in. Pick a day when it's in a sign you resonate with or that corresponds to spell work you'd like to use your moonwater for. The waxing moon in a fire sign is going to give a much different vibe than a dark moon in a water sign.

- Write out your intention, and place it under the vessel of water while it charges.

- Use it to give your pleasure garden (see Taurus season)

a little extra moon magick. Water the plants directly with your moonwater, or put some in a spray bottle and give them a ceremonial spritz!

- Make a magickal tea, and use it to concoct an herbal potion to imbibe!

- Cleanse your waterproof crystals with it! Just be careful. Selenite, and other minerals ending in -ite, are NOT to be submerged in water, since they can lose their luster, rust, or even dissolve. But a quick spritz and a thorough drying can be done every once in a while. You can also easily Google which crystals can be cleansed with water and which can't.

- Add moonwater to your bathing ritual by pouring it into a bath or over your head in the shower. (See Scorpio season for more bath ritual ideas.)

FUN WITH ALCHEMY! MAKING A HYDROSOL

Now I have to admit, not much else makes me feel witchy AF like making a hydrosol. A hydrosol is basically a scented water with healing properties made from distilling fresh herbs and/or flowers into steam and then cooling the steam into liquid again. The most common example is rosewater, but you can make hydrosols out of many different kinds of plants.

FUN FACT: Liquors like gin, vodka, rum, and tequila are all distilled, which places them in the category of "spirits." They are technically made from steam.

Perfect for water-worshipping Cancer season, making a hydrosol utilizes all forms of water (liquid, ice, and vapor) and mimics the alchemical operation of distillation. This process of boiling and condensing psychic material purifies it of ego and id so your highest mind can shine brightly. As with all of the alchemical operations, the hands-on piece relates to an inner process meant to increase self-awareness. You can keep that in mind as you go, or just have some fun making magick water!

If smells aren't super important to you, feel free to use whatever plant materials you would like. Some common plants to work with are rose, lavender, orange blossom, and mint.

You can use hydrosols in a variety of ways, but they are most commonly used in skin care. They carry all the benefits of essential oils but are diluted enough to be safe for topical use. They make great toners and hydration sprays and are anti-inflammatory.

ACCESSORIES

- 1 large pot with lid
- 1 large heat-safe bowl
- 1 smaller heat-safe bowl (This will collect your hydrosol, so make sure it's nice and clean.)
- Ice (Okay, I'm not going to lie, you are going to need a lot of ice.)
- 1 large plastic sealable bag (A Ziploc freezer bag is perfect.)
- Spring or filtered water (This is one place where I will tell you not to cut corners—don't use tap water!)
- 5 cups of fresh herbs and/or flowers
- 1 amber glass bottle

STEP 1: Place your large heat-safe bowl upside-down in the center of the large pot. This is going to act like a platform for the second smaller bowl, which will sit on top of it, right side up. The small bowl is where the distilled steam will collect, creating the purified hydrosol.

STEP 2: Arrange the fresh plant material around the sides of the larger upside-down bowl (not in it). Pour your filtered or spring water over the plant material until it is covered but the water level is still below the top of the larger bowl; otherwise the small bowl will start to float.

STEP 3: Place the large pot lid upside-down to cover the top of the pot. Fill the plastic bag with ice, seal it, and place it on top of the lid of the pot.

STEP 4: Boil the water, then gently simmer it for thirty minutes to four hours, depending on how much hydrosol you want to make! As you go, replace the bag of ice every time it melts down to water, which will be fairly often, so keep your eyes on it!

STEP 5: Remove the pot from the heat, and remove the lid. Behold! Your small bowl is now filled with magick water! Notice how clear and fragrant it is! Are you in love?!

STEP 6: Carefully pour the hydrosol into an amber glass bottle, and store it in the fridge or another place that stays cool and dark. A properly stored hydrosol can last for months!

"HEX THE HEAT WAVE" COOLING SPRAY

Let's use our newfound skills to make a cooling mist for the dog days of Cancer season. Use it to cool down skin, soothe sunburns, or spray your pillow for a chill summer slumber.

ACCESSORIES
- One 2-ounce glass bottle
- 1 ounce mint hydrosol (Use peppermint or spearmint as your fresh herb. You can also add basil, lavender, or rosemary.)
- 1 ounce witch hazel
- A few drops of mint, basil, or lavender essential oil (optional)
- Essence of a blue crystal [1]

STEP 1: Fill the glass bottle about halfway with the hydrosol.

STEP 2: Fill the rest of the bottle, *almost* to the top, with witch hazel, and shake to combine.

STEP 3: Add a few drops of mint, basil, or lavender essential oil if you want to amplify the scent.

STEP 4: Add a few drops of essence of a blue crystal, or simply place your bottled hydrosol next to a blue crystal for a few hours to charge.

STEP 5: Store in the fridge, and spray on your face and body when you need to cool down and chill out!

---

1   As done in the essence-making process in Taurus season, place the blue crystal next to a glass bowl filled with spring water. Set the bowl in a spot where it will get full sun for at least four hours. Strain, and mix that water with an equal amount of brandy or vegetable glycerin. Some crystals can be placed directly in water, but some will dissolve, so I like the "indirect method" of placing the crystal close enough to the glass that it's touching without being in the water itself.

POWER-SHOWER SALT SCRUB

Something to know about me is that I love, love, love a body scrub. I love how soft and smooth it makes my skin feel, but I also love to use scrubs as a ritual tool. It's probably one of my fave ritual tools, if I'm being honest, since it's so efficient. If I've had a long, draining day or a weird encounter, I love to use a magickal scrub in the shower to send that energy (and dry skin) down the drain. Or, if I have something fun or important to do, I'll use a scrub to make sure I'm at my most radiant. The best news is that it's super simple (and cheap!) to make your own, and when you DIY, you can infuse all kinds of magick as you go! Since Cancer season is strongly correlated with the ocean, it's the perfect time to incorporate the healing power of salt.

ACCESSORIES

- 1 cup salt (Choose a special salt rather than table salt. Sea salt will do, if the grains are fine enough not to exfoliate too much and cause pain! My favorite is Epsom salts, which soothe sore muscles as well. You can also mix a couple of kinds of salts.)
- ¼ cup carrier oil (Many types of oil will work. The most

common are jojoba oil, olive oil, avocado oil, grapeseed oil, and sweet almond oil. You can definitely be intentional here, or just use what you already have!)

- 10 to 20 drops of your favorite essential oil (Let your magickal creativity go wild. Pick a scent or two that smell clearing or fresh to you.)
- 1 tablespoon intentional ingredients (optional). Sprinkle a few pinches of dried herbs, one or two drops of a flower or gem essence (see Taurus season), or a moonwater that corresponds with your magickal workings. Just be careful not to change the consistency by adding too much liquid.
- 1 medium-sized bowl
- 1 glass jar (for storage)

STEP 1: Choose a moon phase and a sign to work with, and charge all of your ingredients under it, including the bowl and jar, for a few hours or overnight.

STEP 2: Hold each ingredient in your hands for a few moments, and infuse it with your intention.

STEP 3: Put everything in the bowl and stir intentionally! Clockwise for waxing, glow-up vibes and counterclockwise for waning, clearing vibes.

STEP 4: Now transfer everything to the jar, and you're ready to go! Bonus points if you decorate the jar. You could make a mini vision board as a label or even just tie some ribbon around the top in a color to match your spell (see Leo season for more color magick).

STEP 5: You're ready to scrub! Hopefully you've already infused your scrub with a lot of intention, but it couldn't hurt to hold it in your hands and do some quick visualization around your desired outcome right before you actually apply it. You could even make up a rhyme, or borrow one of mine, like "Scrub of mine, help me shine!" or "With salt and moon, I'll be clear soon."

SHELL SPELL FOR SURRENDER

While crystals like moonstone correspond to Cancer, I always associate this season with seashells. These magickal little treasures can teach us a lot if we let them.

A few years ago, I was on a beautiful beach looking for seashells. Despite living on the coast and always combing the shore, I'd never really found what I would deem a "perfect seashell," or even one that was fully intact. Until I saw Seline. There she was, a perfect cream-colored little conch, and I loved her instantly. What a prize! What a souvenir! I doted on her like the treasure she was. She gave me her name! We even took some selfies together! A few hours later, lying in the sand, resting Seline on my chest, I decided to ask her a question. "What wisdom do I need from the universe right now?"

I held her up to my ear, and you know what she said?

"Throw me back."

Obviously, I was devastated, but the "voice" was clear as could be. Bummed, I reflected on why *this* was her message. I thought about how it related to my life, as it was a particularly stressful time and I was really suffering. There were things that were spiraling out of my control, but grasping at them was creating so much anxiety. The message as I received it spoke to letting go and surrendering attachments. The idea of non-attachment comes from Buddhist philosophy, and I first learned about it through the twelve-step programs my parents were part of while I was growing up. While I myself am not a Buddhist, I do try to cultivate a practice of non-attachment, especially when I'm reminded by seashells. Since control is an illusion and the only constant is change, the less we attach ourselves to things, thoughts, and outcomes, the more peace and serenity we'll find. Good, bad, or ugly, our attachments can really keep us from our spiritual path.

So, the more I thought about it, I knew this was the lesson for me. Of course, Seline didn't want to be kept away from her beautiful home in paradise. Nor would I! In fact, I believe holding on to her would've caused harm. So after a few days of hanging out and appreciating her beauty and energy, I threw her back into the ocean, as far as I could.

Honestly, it was really hard, but it made me feel good. As a rule of thumb, I find that generally, the harder a thing is to do, the more it is also the right thing to do.

I think about Seline all the time. I hope she's floating free in gorgeous, warm tropical waters, as she has for hundreds or maybe thousands of years. She reminds me that you can hold something without controlling it, without attaching to it, and I'm grateful for that reminder every day.

Next time you find a shell or another tiny treasure out in nature, ask it if it has a message for you. Spend some time with it if you need to, but return it to its home environment before the end of the moon cycle. Think about what else you can surrender and detach from in your life, and LET IT GOOOOOOOOOOOOO!

CRAB-WALK CLOTHING SWAP

Let's round out Cancer season by taking some inspiration straight from the source—crabs! Hermit crabs in particular. Like, did you know that hermit crabs trade shells when they outgrow them? Seriously! When a new shell appears on the beach, hermit crabs line up according to size and swap shells, each going up in size to give themselves room to grow. As Carl Engelking writes in *Discover* magazine, "This chain reaction is called a vacancy chain, and it's an ingenious way for the creatures to survive while sharing limited resources." Seriously, search "hermit crab shell swap" on YouTube, and watch in wonder.

In her amazing book *Emergent Strategy*, genius of our time and activist extraordinaire adrienne maree brown outlines ways that we can use strategies learned from our plant and animal neighbors to cultivate community and create change in the world. Concepts like biomimicry (which is exactly what it sounds like) and interdependence show how nature can help us solve the complex web of issues facing humankind today. She writes:

Humans are unique because we compete when it isn't necessary. We could reason our way to more sustainable processes, but we use our intelligence to outsmart each other. . . . The idea of interdependence is that we can meet each other's needs in a variety of ways, that we can truly lean on others and they can lean on us. It means we have to decentralize our ideas of where solutions and decisions happen, where ideas come from.

So what the heck does this have to do with you? Well, you can organize a shell-swap of your very own, except with clothes!

The idea of a clothing swap (again, exactly what it sounds like) is to bring some sustainability practices to your closet. The fashion industry, "fast fashion" in particular, creates an enormous amount of waste that is contributing to destructive climate change in a major way. A clothing swap is one of many ways that you can be part of the solution instead of the problem.

Organize your swap on any scale you like! Have a few friends over, and ask them to clean out their closets beforehand. Everybody lays out what they brought, and then you all go "shopping"! It's okay if you're not all the same size or shape. Someone I consider very stylish, Leanne Ford, encourages people who like her lewks to shop in any department and try on any size. What's important is how a garment looks on you. "I never look at size, and I'm full rein: guys', girls', boys' clothes, men's, any of it, I just pay attention to how things fit on me."

Here are some more tips:

- Ask folks to bring gently worn clothing and accessories that they no longer use.
- Decide in advance if you want to limit the number of items people bring or take. You could do it "bring what you have, take what you need" style, or set a limit of five to fifteen items per person to keep it more manageable.
- Organize piles or racks by type of garment (dresses, tops, bottoms, accessories, and so on).
- Ask people to bring garments on hangers if you have a place to hang things up, as well as a tote for taking their treasures home.
- Designate a space for trying items on, or ask folks to wear

leggings and tanks so they can try things on over them.

- Provide a full-length mirror if possible.
- Make it a party! Provide snacks and drinks and tunes, or ask folks to BYOB.
- Decide where to donate leftover items (I encourage you to seek out nonprofits in your area where the clothes will be used by their clients, instead of a big-box thrift store).

Feeling bold? Organize a swap open to the public. A good friend of mine (a shout-out to Liz Gardner-Carr of Eleventh House Vintage!) hosts community clothing swaps that are a huge hit. It's a lot of work though, so make sure you have the bandwidth for something on that scale.

You don't have to stick to just clothes either. At one of the community clothing swaps, we had our own "Witch Switch" table, where folks could trade ritual tools that they're no longer working with for something else.

You can expand this idea to any kind of resource! There are also lots of "buy nothing" community groups on social media that emulate this idea. The important thing is to focus on sharing community resources in a way that encourages sustainability!

Ready to come up for air and into the light, my little crabs? Get ready to see and be seen as we head into Leo season!

Leo Season

Solar Flair

July 23–August 22

- **SYMBOL:** The Lion
- **DEITY/PLANET:** The Sun
- **ELEMENT:** Fire

- **TAROT SUIT:** Wands
- **BODY CONNECTION:** Heart
- **CRYSTAL:** Citrine, pyrite

Leo season is about being ALIVE. It's about being seen. Glowing up, showing up, and LIVING OUT LOUD. Now is the time for cultivating main character energy and expressing yourself boldly. It's sunshine and selfies. I mean, three of the four most-followed people on Instagram have major Leo placements in their birth charts, and the other one is literally named Leo.[1] Need I say more? (Well, I'm obviously going to!)

Now, all seasons have celebrities born under that sign, but Leo season is the time of superstars. Madonna, JLo, Barack Obama, Whitney Houston, Mick Jagger, and Meghan Markle are just a few examples of Leo suns who exude star power from every pore. They're not just famous, they're icons. With their big smiles beaming, their talents on full display, Leos are permanent fixtures on the world stage, and we're gonna hear them roooaarrrr!

But let's back up. How did we get from some distant lights in the sky to the flashbulbs of the paparazzi? Well, let's start with an ancient popularity contest of sorts. Leo the lion constellation

---

1   At the time of writing, Cristiano Ronaldo is #1 with a Leo moon; Leo Messi is #2; Selena Gomez, #3, is a Leo Rising, with Mercury, Venus, and Chiron also in Leo; and Kylie Jenner, who in my opinion oozes Leo energy, is #4, with a Leo sun.

is one of the brightest in the night sky and is visible almost everywhere on earth. Appearing during the hottest time of year in the Northern Hemisphere, Leo season has always been associated with the height of summertime, a time of abundance. For example, for the ancient Egyptians it coincided with the flooding of the Nile each year, which provided the irrigation needed to turn the dry desert into a fertile oasis. In Europe the harvest festival Lammas, traditionally held on August 1, marks the halfway point between the Summer Solstice and the Fall Equinox. An offering of a loaf of bread from the year's first harvest is given as an abundance spell for further harvests. So, from the time of our earliest civilizations to the present day, the big, bright lion in the sky means happy days are here again.

Speaking of being the center of the universe, Leo's ruling "planet" is the sun. In addition to literally *giving us life*, the sun is associated with vitality, generosity, expansiveness, warmth, and enthusiasm. Leo also rules over the heart, which gives life to our body and our passions. So it's not just vanity that leaves these lions with a sense of central importance.

This month is all about channeling your inner celebrity. Pretending you're the star of your own reality show (or docuseries, if you're highbrow). Your playlists become soundtracks. Your outfits become costumes. Don't walk down the street, strut. Smile big, toothy smiles. Be a legend in your own mind! We're going to soak up some sun, open our hearts, and create our own personal solar system!

THE GLAMOROUS MAGICK OF SHOWING UP

GOLD SUN MEDITATION

Did you know that we all have access to our own personal sun? It's true! Its vibration is gold, it lives right above our heads, and it is filled with our most radiant life-force energy. The best part? It's all ours. It holds the energy of our souls, our higher selves. It's not about good or bad energy, it's about *your* energy, which is neutral and healing. Cultivating neutrality is a powerful psychic tool that creates a sense of inner spaciousness, which allows us to release resistance, stay present, and operate with more compassion toward ourselves and others. So try not to place judgment on what your energy looks or feels like, and just trust that the way to be most effective in your life is to be centered in your own neutral, golden energy.

Since our energy becomes attached to other people, places, and things all the time, one of my absolute favorite psychic tools is connecting with my gold sun in meditation, calling my own energy back in an empowering way. So if the idea of taking center stage freaks you out a bit, or if you're just feeling a little drained, let your gold sun help you sparkle and shine this season.

1. Start by dropping a grounding cord, to connect yourself with the earth. (See Introduction.)
2. Now visualize a gold sun floating two to three feet above your head.
3. Use this brilliant gold sun as a magnet, pulling your personal golden light back from all directions.

4. Patiently watch as this light fills your sun. Let it take as long as it needs.

5. When your sun is full to bursting, imagine the golden light spilling out like a sun shower around you. Let the warm light fill your physical and energetic body, from your head to your toes.

6. Once you feel recharged, gently come out of meditation and offer some gratitude to your sun.

CULTIVATE A CONFIDENCE COSTUME

Leo season is the perfect time to focus on things that may be considered "superficial" but can be absolutely crucial to our self-esteem. Maybe how we appear on the outside "shouldn't" be important, but we all know that it is. Now trust me, I'm not talking about trying to adhere to oppressive norms, or ridiculous standards of beauty. I'm talking about using your personal style to tap into your own fullest expression of identity. There are lots of ways to use glamour magick to feel like your highest and best self.

Wearing special ceremonial clothing and jewelry to represent and channel specific energies has pretty much always been a thing. This attention to adornment is timeless. Royalty have their crowns and cloaks, militaries have medals, punks have pins, and the rest of us have jewelry, outfits, hairdos, makeup, and tattoos. Glamour magick is traditionally about using illusion to change one's appearance, but we're going to do something

a little different: tap into the most empowering way to use what you've already got to show up anywhere feeling like your best self.

Having lived most of my life in scarcity, I dreamt of the day that I would be resourced enough to have what I deemed "the perfect outfit" for any occasion. It didn't mean that the clothes had to be expensive or flashy; I just wanted stuff that fit well, felt good, and matched the energy I was trying to bring. As a highly sensitive person, I have sensory issues that make it hard to feel comfortable in certain fabrics and textures, so I have to consider more than just appearance when I shop for clothes. (In fact I now prioritize how something feels over how it looks on me. There is no sweater too soft and no garment too shapeless, as far as I'm concerned!) As I've gotten older and more financially stable, I've been able to invest in things that meet all of those criteria and assist me in looking how I want to look. It's been a real game-changer, when it comes to having the confidence to step into a more visible version of myself for my career. The part of my birth chart that is ruled by Leo is called the Midheaven, which corresponds directly to vocation and self-image. Because being HausWitch sometimes puts me center stage on social media, in interviews and photo shoots, and when getting the word out for my books (wink wink) and taking up leadership roles, as a natural introvert, I really lean into that Leo Midheaven for support. When I need to get into character, I wear my bright-red lipstick and black-framed glasses, kind of like Clark Kent and Superman. When I'm not wearing those things, I feel like Erica, but when I put them on, I feel like HausWitch, and it's an important distinction.

So while clothes definitely don't "make the [hu]man" we

can use some wardrobe witchery to help ourselves feel like the special little sunbeams we are!

1. **GO THROUGH YOUR CLOSET.** Separate out your favorite things, the ones that make you look and feel your best. These are your "power pieces." (Avoid items that are favorites for other reasons, like nostalgia, expense, or showiness.) Do you notice any patterns? Is there a consistent color palette or fabric family? Are loose, airy garments your go-to, or do you feel best showing off your shape in form-fitting clothes? Let these observations inform how to work with your current wardrobe and curate your shopping. When you feel good, you look good.

2. **TAKE SOME INSPIRATION FROM MAGICK!** Be inspired by a tarot card or your favorite crystal, plant ally, pet, or celestial body. Think the Queen of Swords is a badass? (She is!) Let her inspire your lewk. But don't feel like you have to take this advice literally. You don't have to have a cloud cape and a crown to embody the energies of clarity and emotional mastery that she represents. Heck, even your zodiac sign or the astrological season you're in could serve as inspiration. I like to say my Scorpio Rising is my "cool girl" outfit (think black leather jacket, sunglasses, and IDGAF energy).

3. **CREATE A PERFORMER PERSONA.** Sometimes fairly shy, introverted folks come to work at my shop. It comes with the territory, since many of us are highly sensitive, intuitive, and empathic people. We don't have a dress code, so it can be harder for people

to separate their private self from the one who has to interact with the public, and over the years we've had to coach a few of those folks out of their shells so they could provide good customer service. Something that we have found really effective is encouraging people to come up with a persona. Now, this doesn't involve anything psychologically rigorous; you're really tapping into your extroverted side (everyone has one!) using clothing, accessories, and attitude to "get into character." People who have worked in the service industry already know this: you have to have a customer service voice, mannerisms, and above all a rock-solid relationship with humility to do those jobs. So why not have some fun with it?! This idea reaches beyond

work. A performer persona can come in handy any time you feel intimidated by something you have to do.

4. **USE COLOR MAGICK.** Speaking of showing up! Colors are literally visible light. Using color to aid in expression is as old as humanity itself. From red ochre cave paintings to royal-purple cloaks, color as a form of magick has been used to decorate, distinguish, and inspire in every culture around the world. Intentionally working with color through makeup, clothes, and jewelry is one of the easiest ways to incorporate a little witchcraft into the everyday.

Most color correspondence charts will tell you that red stands for this and yellow stands for that. If those traditional associations feel good to you, go with them. Use them to help you figure out makeup and nail polish spells, wardrobe spells, or what crystals to wear as jewelry to achieve your desired magickal or sartorial outcome.

For me, colors have really personal meanings that I incorporate into my wardrobe-related spells. For example, bright red is the color of my ultimate confidence costume, my lipstick Lady Danger. But it also reminds me of my beloved father, who loved the color red. So when I wear red, not only am I calling in an energy of confidence, but I'm calling in support from my guardian angel. Purple is my favorite color, but I didn't

wear it a lot until I was formally introduced to my spirit guide that embodies that color (see Gemini season). Now I frequently wear purple nail polish as a tribute. I think we all have a distinct relationship with color, and magick is always more powerful when it is close to your heart.

What color is your favorite song? What color comes to mind when you think of your friends? What color reminds you of your favorite place or your personal hero? Those are just a few prompts to get you thinking about your own relationships to colors. Use this chart to help map out your own personal correspondences to color.

Clothing glamour spells are just the beginning in terms of using color magick. Think of all the ways you can utilize color to bring different energies into your life. Your home, your rituals, and your hobbies can all be intentionally colorful!

COLOR	TRADITIONAL	PERSONAL (WRITE IN)
Red	Passion, courage, action	
Orange	Creativity, vitality, inspiration	
Yellow	Joy, illumination, determination	
Green	Growth, abundance, generosity	
Blue	Healing, harmony, serenity	
Purple	Spirituality, magick, purpose	
Pink	Self-love, friendship, devotion	
White	Cleansing, peace, clarity	
Gray	Balance, reflection, composure	
Brown	Grounding, stability, security	
Black	Protection, sophistication, transformation	

SUN SPELLS

"SOAK UP THE SUN" SOLAR INFUSIONS

You know how everything just feels a little easier in summer? Well, using the sun to brew tea really speaks to me as a gesture of welcoming a sense of ease, releasing effort, and letting nature take the wheel. Sun tea is usually served over ice as a refreshing treat on lazy summer days. Instead of steeping tea in boiling water, we're going to ask the sun to heat the water slowly over the course of an afternoon. It's very easy to make a basic sun tea, and also very easy to experiment and improvise, creating your own delicious and medicinal magickal blends. Or you can use some of my favorite concoctions described in this section.

Do this spell on a Sunday for some added oomph, but any sunny day will do! You'll need

3 to 4 hours. I usually set a timer for 3 hours, 33 minutes, because I'm an angel number girly, but you could also use your own auspicious timing to add magick. Just don't brew your tea for longer than 4 hours, to reduce any risk of bacteria forming. Use these basic directions for any of the spells that follow.

1. Gather your vessel(s). You definitely want to use glass jars with lids, and you want them to be squeaky-clean and sanitary. (Don't use plastic!) I recommend using small jars (twelve to sixteen ounces) for single servings and larger jars (thirty-two to sixty-four ounces) for making whole batches.

2. The general rule is to use six ounces of tea for every cup of water. At times I have played it very fast and loose

with this. In my first go-around, I literally just threw handfuls of herbs into a jar, and the tea came out great! But by all means measure if you're a precision witch.

3. Curate your magickal herbs. Tap into some inner-child energy and "pretend" you're a woods witch brewing a magickal potion. Set an intention to infuse into your tea. You can use fresh or dried herbs and flowers from your pleasure garden (see Taurus season), or regular store-bought tea bags. Or a combination! Some blends lend themselves to a tasty tea (mint, lemon balm, basil), while others may be more about the medicine (yarrow, nettles, echinacea). You decide!

4. If using fresh herbs, make sure to rinse them well. There is a slim chance that they will harbor bacteria. If you're nervous about that, just stick to dried.

5. Fill your sacred sun jar(s) with water (room temperature or warm), and add the tea ingredients. If you're using loose tea, make sure to stir it up a bit; if you're using bags, make sure they are fully submerged (but leave the string outside the jar).

6. Place the jar outside, in full sun. If you have a really sunny windowsill, that should work just fine too! Once you've found a good spot, wrap your hands around the jar, and meditate for a moment on your intention. Let the ingredients you chose help guide you.

7. Keep your jar tightly sealed throughout the process, especially if it is sitting outside. Check on your tea a few times while it brews.

Watch how it changes color and transforms. You could even do a little tea-gazing by unfocusing your eyes and trying to "read the water."

8. After three to four hours, grab your jar and strain your tea through cheesecloth or a fine-mesh strainer. Put it back in the jar, and refrigerate the tea immediately.

9. Once it has cooled, pour it over ice and enjoy a glass of herbal sundrops! Thank the sun for its vibrancy and illumination! Drink your tea within a few days.

JUST TO BE EXTRA

- Honey, simple syrup, or fresh fruit will add to the taste of your tea, but don't add it during the brewing process. Sugar can encourage bacteria growth. Instead, add any such ingredient before popping the tea in the fridge or right before you are going to drink it.

- If you really want to show off, why not use some of those pretty ice cubes we made in Taurus season?

- Try these recipes with moonwater you made the night before. Or add a few drops of a gem or flower essence to the jar.

- You can make single-serve jars for having friends over. Everyone gets their own spell in a jar! Add fresh fruit to "make it nice," and keep the tea on ice.

Here are a few of my favorite sun tea recipes. As with anything you plan to ingest, make sure to Google any ingredients you are less familiar with, and pay attention to caffeine content, especially if you're pregnant.

"OPEN YOUR HEART (TO ME)" HIBISCUS TEA

I love hibiscus tea, and I love making it in the sun because it creates the most beautiful deep-magenta color. It's also heart-opening and good for connecting with feelings of self-love and compassion.

ACCESSORIES

- ½ cup dried hibiscus petals
- A few dried rosebuds
- 2 cinnamon sticks
- ¼ cup lime juice
- ¼ cup raw honey
- Lime wedges or fresh mint (optional)

1. Place hibiscus, rosebuds, and cinnamon sticks in your jar. Fill with 7 cups of filtered water. Follow previous directions for steeping.

2. After steeping, add lime juice and honey to the jar.

3. Give the mixture a little shake, to make sure the honey dissolves. Then refrigerate the tea.

4. Garnish with a lime wedge or fresh mint if you'd like, and enjoy!

"LION IN THE SUN" RELAXING CHAMOMILE TEA

ACCESSORIES

- 1 part dried chamomile flowers
- 1 part dried passion fruit flowers
- 1 part dried lavender

Combine all ingredients in the jar and fill with filtered water. Steep and refrigerate. Then find yourself a shady spot, curl up, and relax with this catnap-inducing blend.

"TOO FRESH TO BE STRESSED" MINT MOJI TEA

ACCESSORIES

- Mint tea bags or loose dried mint
- Fresh lime juice
- Fresh mint leaves, muddled
- Simple syrup

1. Make sun tea with loose dried mint or mint tea bags and filtered water.

2. After steeping, add a little fresh lime juice, muddled mint leaves, and some simple syrup for sweetness. All the flavors of a mojito, without the alcohol!

SIMPLE SUN SPELLS

Did you know that exposing just the palms of your hands to the
sun for fifteen to thirty minutes can give you all the vitamin D your
body needs to keep making it? Vitamin D is really important, since
a deficiency can lead to depression, insomnia, and muscle fatigue,
among other stuff that makes you feel icky. So whether you're
a porcelain doll like me, or just trying to limit the amount of UV light
that hits your skin, this little hack could be really helpful. While you're
there, you could take a look at a palmistry chart and see what's up with
your Apollo and heart lines!

SUNSHINE IN A BOTTLE SPRAY

This might be the easiest way ever to bring some sunshine with you
after Leo season is over and sunbeams are scarce. It's the exact same
process used to make moonwater (see Cancer season), but with the
sun. This time, bottle it up and use it to spritz yourself whenever you
need a jolt of brightness.

- Place a glass bowl of filtered
  water in direct sunlight for
  four hours.
- Fill a two- to four-ounce glass
  bottle with the water.

- Make an essence of
  sunflower, marigold, or
  chamomile, and add a few
  drops to the bottle.
- Make an essence of citrine,
  carnelian, or pyrite (indirect

method only), and add a few drops of that.

- Last, find essential oils that feel bright and fresh, like orange or lemon, and add a few drops of those.

I wouldn't add too much because we want the spray to feel light and fresh, not overpowering.

- Shake and spray on a rainy day!

"MOMENT IN THE SUN" CYANOTYPE FUN

One of the coolest ways I've found to work with the sun is with sun-printing. Cyanotyping is the fancy name, and it means working with the UV rays of the sun to imprint shapes and designs on sensitized paper or fabric. A special emulsion allows for monochrome images to appear when it is washed away after the printing process. It's basically tan lines, but instead of your swimsuit blocking your skin from getting darker in certain places, you use different types of objects to keep the paper or fabric from getting "tan" in certain places. Which can result in some really beautiful designs! Leaves and greenery are some of the most popular items to work with, but anything with a defined shape will work. You can even cut shapes out of paper, but you may want to stick them down or put a piece of glass over them to keep everything flat and in place.

It's very easy and inexpensive to source cyanotype paper or fabric, and to DIY emulsion. A quick Google search or trip to your local art supply store will yield a variety of results. I've

even found paper in a range of different colors in addition to the standard blue. ("Cyanotype" means "dark-blue impression.")

Once you've gathered your cyanotype material and objects, simply lay the paper down outside on a flat surface that gets a lot of sun, emulsion side up (you'll be able to tell which side is which). Then place your objects on the paper in an intentional way. You could even create a mandala if you're feeling ambitious!

Need some ideas for objects? Here are a few:

Feathers
Crystals with interesting shapes
Shells
Wishbones
Flowers
Letters

After ten to fifteen minutes (or whatever time the instructions indicate for your particular paper or fabric), rinse your material under a faucet until the water runs clear. Lay it in the sun to dry!

This process is a great way to embrace the concept of being in co-creation with the universe, so it would make a great manifesting spell. You could use objects to symbolize the intention you'd like to draw in.

Then keep the art you created on your altar while you wait to see how your spell turns out!

Seriously though, don't overthink this. Just have fun! Because I've enjoyed experimenting with it so much, I try not to put pressure on myself to come up with the coolest design or most thought-out spell. Remember, sometimes things are just meant to be fun, not productive!

ANIMAL RIGHTS AND REWILDING YOUR WORLD

Since lions are known for being the "king of the jungle," let's talk about animal sovereignty. I think most of us can agree that animals are living, breathing, sentient beings. Sentience refers to having the capacity, awareness, and cognitive ability to feel. Early human hunter-gatherer groups revered and respected animals, not just as equals but in some cases as superiors. However, since the earliest days of human civilization, the process of domestication has created a murky relationship between people and their animals. The more that animals have become intertwined with our human world, the more we ask them to fit into the way humans do things. Which, as you can probably imagine, is not really how wild animals want to do things.

Here in the "West," early Judeo-Christian thought leaders decided that animals have no souls of their own, do not feel pain, and are here to serve humans, so we basically have full dominion to do whatever we want to them.[2] Animals have no souls? They can't feel pain? Seriously though, *what?!* Nonetheless, this mindset has informed the way we've treated animals for far too long. It has made possible things like factory farming, a bane on the climate and (I would argue) humanity

2   Like, honestly, don't even get me started on these guys. Everyone from Augustine and Thomas Aquinas to Descartes and Kant had some pretty disturbing ideas that have been normalized over the centuries. And not just toward animals.

itself. Circuses, zoos (sorry), rodeos, and even horse-drawn carriages are examples of the ways in which animals are made to act against their nature, separated from their families in captivity, for our enjoyment. Case in point: there are animal rescues and sanctuaries that focus on helping animals *recover* from that kind of toil and torment all over the world.

I know this stuff is super tough to think about, and I promise I'm not trying to terrorize you like that Sarah McLachlan ASPCA commercial from the early 2000s. But Leo season is the perfect time to lead with the heart, cultivate compassion, and act with courage. My wife, a Leo, really opened my eyes to a more animal-centric way of looking at the world. I will never forget the first time I watched a costume drama featuring a big battle on horseback with her. As soon as

the horses appeared on screen, she said, "Awwww, poor horses."

Confused, I said, "Well, those horses are just actors, nothing bad is going to happen to them!"

Her reply: "Do you think horses want to be actors?"

The answer was clear. No, I don't think horses want to be actors. I don't think they want to be in battles either. I think they want to frolic in a field with their families. If you don't believe me, Google any random animal and the phrase "set free after captivity" or "reunited with their [cub, friend, mother, herd]." Then have yourself a nice ugly cry.

While we can't entirely shut down factory farming and animal testing labs (yet), we can still support and spread the word about animal sentience in little ways every day. We just need to unlearn the moral ambivalence that allows us to pamper and protect some animals, while treating others as chattel.

What positive steps can we take to rewild our world? Well, of course the big thing is to advocate for animal sentience laws around the world. The UK passed the Animal Welfare (Sentience) Act in 2022, which recognizes animal sentience and the moral obligation to protect and care for these creatures. France, New Zealand, and Peru all have similar laws, and while this type of legislation is picking up steam around the world, the laws don't always lend themselves to practical enforcement. (Some places recognize animal sentience but don't regulate farming, fishing, or hunting animals.) In our country a few states have animal sentience laws, but there's nothing at the federal level.

We can also think about the way we eat and make different, more ethical choices.[3] We can encourage our friends to adopt pets from shelters instead of shopping for them from breeders. After all, breeding animals is kind of where this whole issue started. While breeding animals for food makes some practical sense, breeding them to have funny legs and smushed faces seems pretty sinister when you consider that those animals often suffer from deformities and other consequences due to genetic manipulation. You can even stop killing bugs in your home and respect that, really, we're in their territory. I am deathly afraid of spiders, but you won't catch me killing them! (Plus, they keep other bugs away!)

---

3   Now before you ask, yes, I eat meat. As much as I am an advocate for acknowledging and defending animal sentience, I am not perfect at it. I do try to eat only ethically sourced meat and have been steadily decreasing my meat consumption in general over the past few years. All this to say that we're all on our own journeys, and no one is perfect when they start. In any case, I hope my transparency here makes me seem like less of a hypocrite.

But perhaps the most accessible place to start is with our own little Haus lions, tigers, and wolves. We can recalibrate our relationships with our pets. Now, a lot of us feel like our pets live really charmed lives. They sleep all day! They don't have to worry about finding food! They don't have to pay taxes or rent! Though these things may be true, they are not necessarily in line with an animal-centric life. For example: My cat Salem is *my baby*, and I treat her as such. I'm sure a lot of you can relate. I've had her since she was eight weeks old (she's almost eleven years old at the time I'm writing this), and we are extremely bonded. But when I intentionally connect to her, she tells me that she doesn't want to be treated like a baby. She wants to be treated like my bestie, who happens to be a cat. So though I still slip into some baby talk with her (what, am I made of stone?!), I do try to treat her more like her own "purrrson," instead of trying to impose a human mother-child dynamic. Rather than forcing

affection on her, I try to pay attention to her body language and respect her spatial boundaries. I don't need her to explain to me in English that her flicking tail means "Fuck right off." Lastly, after the great panda-hat incident of Christmas 2017, I never, ever make her wear clothes.

In an incredibly thought-provoking article on ethical pet ownership, Kenny Torella explores the mindset of good people who still have room for improvement around centering their pet's true animal nature:

We demand companionship with as little friction as possible, expecting our pets (especially dogs) to be docile and agreeable, and to adapt quickly to the human world, with its countless rules and norms that mean nothing to them. And then when they inevitably fail to do so at first, we deem their natural habits misbehavior in need of correction, or abandonment.

There is an exercise for psychically connecting to your pet in my first book, *HausMagick*, but here we're gonna open our hearts and go a little deeper. We're going to get down on their level, do some heart-opening yoga poses, and try to put ourselves in their shoes, I mean, their paws!

"WILD AT HEART" HEART-OPENING RITUAL

1. Start out in child's pose, *balasana* in Sanskrit: Kneel, then rest your butt on your heels. Bend all the way forward, so your forehead touches the floor. Rest your arms down alongside you.

2. Close your eyes and take some deep breaths. If you'd like, you can try to make a psychic connection with your pet, simply by mentally greeting them and letting them know you're listening.

3. Next, move into sphinx pose, *salamba bhujangasana*, by lying on your stomach, with your elbows directly under your shoulder blades. Then press firmly into the legs from the tops of your feet, all the way up to your thighs. Then lift the upper body.

4. Take a few breaths here to connect to your heart and visualize it expanding.

5. Look around from this pet's-eye view. See the world through your pet's eyes for a few moments.

6. Now move back into child's pose to reset your back. While you're here, take some more deep breaths and ask to receive guidance on how to be a better pet parent.

7. When you're ready, sit up and write down anything that comes to mind. This is probably your pet communicating with you. Maybe they want to switch up their food. Maybe they want a different nickname. Maybe they just want more time with you!

8. If it feels like something deeper is happening, consult a certified pet behaviorist, either online or in person. Much different from animal trainers, behaviorists are educated in science-based animal-centric techniques for helping your pets live their best lives. Just make sure the behaviorist is accredited by a reputable organization like the Animal Behavior Society. The big thing is to stay away from information that encourages punishing your animals, since studies have shown that hitting, yelling, and intimidation don't do much to correct their behavior and may actually make them afraid of you, which is probably the last thing you want!

9. Even if you didn't get any specific messages, hopefully by opening your heart, and literally putting yourselves in their position, you may be inspired to make a few changes in the ways you interact with your pet!

Hopefully you Haus lions have had a nice time basking in the sunbeams, because it's time to get our sh*t together for Virgo season!

Virgo Season

Back to Earth

August 23–September 22

- **SYMBOL:** The Virgin
- **DEITY/PLANET:** Mercury
- **ELEMENT:** Earth
- **TAROT SUIT:** Pentacles
- **BODY CONNECTION:** Digestive system
- **CRYSTAL:** Red jasper, moss agate

For me, Virgo season is always marked by a change in the way the sunlight hits the front of my shop. All of a sudden the brilliant sunbeams of Leo season shift to a softer, more subdued glow, and I don't need a calendar to know that summer is coming to an end. So even though summer *technically* lasts another month, Virgo season isn't so much about *fun in the sun* as winding down and calling back. It ends with the Fall Equinox, and the real shift into cooler days ahead. But don't worry, the rest of summer doesn't have to be a bummer! Reentering routines can be fun! Think of how exciting back-to-school shopping was when you were a kid. Even if the thought of returning to school caused some existential dread, the optimism suggested by a new notebook and a fresh pair of kicks would soften the blow. The chance to reinvent yourself as someone who has their shit *a little bit* more together is the truest vibe of Virgo season. To celebrate, we need to get grounded and dig deep into some nourishing earth magick. But first we need to make a correction . . .

We have to detach ourselves from the patriarchal definition of *virgin* (and everything else, tbh): a woman who hasn't had sexual intercourse. There's nothing like the timeless practice of policing women's bodies to erase the nuance and complexity of the feminine experience. In the mythological context of astrology, a virgin was simply a maiden, or even a goddess. She was thought of as "untouched" because she was self-sufficient, not because she was chaste. In modern terms, she's the babe who's too busy for a boyfriend. She's living, laughing, loving in her carefully curated life and can't be bothered to notice that people are trying to slide into her DMs. Forget purity culture (forever!) and think "Independent Women" by Destiny's Child. (After all, Beyoncé is a Virgo queen herself.)

Like our favorite sign, Gemini ☺, Virgo is ruled by Mercury. Unlike Gemini, Virgo is an earth sign, not an air sign, giving this rulership a different flavor altogether. Still aligned with Mercury's love of information and communication, Virgo shows us a more practical version of these gifts. The way I've heard it described is that Gemini collects information, while Virgo organizes it. But I'm not talking about normal-person organizing—this is virtuoso organizing. It's the kind of organization that's needed in situations where a lot of us just throw our hands in the air and pray someone will do it for us. (Pro tip: hire Virgos!) So this season we're going to channel some of that savant energy to make our lives feel more put together and taken care of. We're slowing down to find the method in the madness and the magick in the mundane.

ACORN AMULETS

When I first moved to Salem from Chicago in 2010, I started a new life, almost from scratch. I didn't know anyone within a thousand-mile radius. I didn't know my way around the area, I didn't have a job to go to, and grad school didn't start for another few months. I desperately needed help grounding myself in my new reality. I was excited about the opportunity to reinvent myself (as someone with their shit *a little bit* more together), but also felt like I couldn't quite find my footing. I turned to my copy of the *Witches' Almanac*, which has a calendar organized by the zodiac seasons, featuring the Moon Signs and vaguely intriguing prompts like "Read the cards" or "Visit the night sea."[1] I decided that one of the ways I could settle into my new life was to use the almanac as my regular calendar and follow as many of these prompts as I could. You might say it was the beginning of my own *intention obsession*. Since I had moved to Salem to study witches and to deepen my own magickal practice, this seemed like the perfect place to start. Appropriately enough, my first directive from the witches was "Carry an acorn for power."

Acorns contain the seeds of oak trees. Usually one acorn has one seed, encapsulated by a shell with a little cap. Only 1 in 10,000 acorns actually becomes a tree, so the other 9,999 are fair game for animals and fungus to feast on. Humans have also eaten acorns for thousands of years, all over the globe, and they are still a part of many Native American cuisines. Once a staple ingredient

---

1   A few years later, when I started the HausWitch blog, I channeled the idea to end each post with a prompt like this one: "The Moon is in [sign] and the Witches say, [prompt]." Eleven years later we still end every one of our newsletters that way.

of the human diet, acorns can be cooked in many different ways. They can be ground into flour to make bread, pressed to make oil, and mashed to make, well, mash. Processing acorns for food is too complicated to get into here, but as with everything else, the internet is vast, and answers abound!

You can also use acorns as a natural fabric dye, producing many shades of rich tans and browns. Once again, this process is a bit too involved to get into here, but if you're up for this challenge, Virgo season is the perfect time for it!

You will need enough acorns to fill a big pot about a third of the way, so always be mindful of how much you are taking from nature and whether it will negatively impact the environment.

Best practice for taking anything from nature: ask for consent, and then make an offering in exchange. I know witches who sing songs, leave a strand of hair, some tobacco, or even a little saliva (but don't rudely spit on a tree, please!) to honor the earth and our bodily connection to it.

For our purposes, I want to invoke acorn magick in some really simple ways. Virgo season is prime time for gathering these little earth seeds in most of the United States. Acorns can be used for all sorts of magickal purposes, from protection to attaining beauty; different witches may offer different ideas. Tap into your intuition to see what magickal workings an acorn or two might assist you with. Don't feel you have to come up with something elaborate! After all, to a city kid like me, just finding an acorn and carrying it in my pocket felt really powerful. Setting an intention, paying close attention to my surroundings, and collecting a ritual ingredient from nature was witchcraft in

and of itself. I ended up simply keeping that acorn on my altar for years.

MORE ACORN IDEAS

- Like any seed, acorns represent fresh starts and new pursuits. Charge an acorn with your intention by decorating it with a nontoxic paint (nail polish would work!) or inscribing it with a symbol or sigil during a new moon. Then plant it (knowing it probably won't grow into an oak tree, but maybe!) or simply keep it on your altar as a reminder of your spell.
- Make a spell pouch to fill with magickal natural ingredients to represent Virgo season. Add herbs, crystals,

or even dirt to harness vibes matching your intention. Then add your acorn to the bag, representing the acorn being buried in earth. Leave it there until you manifest what you desired, or the universe nudges you in another direction.

- Make some cutie Floating Candles.

FLOATING CANDLES

ACCESSORIES

- A dozen or so acorns
- A baking sheet
- 1 candle wick
- Scissors
- 1 wide bowl
- Sand
- Beeswax candle(s)

1. Remove the caps from your acorns, and set them on a baking sheet, empty side up.
2. Bake in the oven at 200°F for an hour to sanitize them. Allow to cool.
3. In the meantime, cut your wick into lengths of one-half inch or one inch, to fit the depth of the acorn caps you are using. (You can use the wick from an unused taper candle. Break it, and remove the wax from around the wick.)
4. Nestle the baked caps in a wide bowl or dish of sand to make sure they stay in place while you're working.
5. Light a beeswax candle, and carefully let the melting wax drip into an acorn top. Continue with each top. (You can, alternatively, melt wax into a vessel that makes it easy to pour the wax into each cap.)

6. Let the wax dry a little, but not too much. Then stick a wick into each cap. The wick should be secured firmly enough stand up on its own. Let the candles cure long enough for the wax to harden.

7. Place a grouping of the candles in a dish, or dishes, of water, and light them! These little guys will burn for ten to twenty minutes, making them perfect for quick rituals and mood lighting.

MUSHROOM MAGICK

As I write this, mushrooms are really having a moment. Not only are actual mushrooms being recognized for their ecological functions and culinary delights (notably as meat substitutes, which is awesome), but symbolic representations of mushrooms are everywhere too. A quick search for "mushroom" on Etsy, the website for handmade and custom gifts, yields over 500,000 results. Clothes, pillows, stickers, tote bags, jewelry, you name it. Swiss psychoanalyst and mystic zaddy Carl Jung would have a field day (or maybe a forest day?) with the symbolism that our collective unconscious is producing when it comes to mushrooms. It's not surprising, considering the important role that mushrooms (and fungi in general) play in regenerating our environment. At a time when trash and toxins are polluting the earth faster than we can talk about it, the fact that there are fungi who eat plastic and break down chemical waste puts these little guys in the realm of superheroes. In fact, for Jungians, within our current cultural moment, the popularity of mushrooms and the Marvel multiverse are related!

Like mushrooms, superheroes are everywhere in popular culture. One might theorize that, with everything overwhelming going on in the world that's making us feel helpless, especially climate change, our collective unconscious is looking for a savior. In the immortal words of Bonnie Tyler, *we need a hero*. Of course, despite what Hollywood is jamming down our throats, it's not realistic to think that Spider-Man or Thor is going to swoop in and save us, but mushrooms just might . . .

Since I myself am not really a mushroom aficionado (I truly wish I was, but I have a strong aversion to anything fungi-related), I enlisted the HausWitch Spell Specialist Paige Curtin to come up with some magickal ways to work with mushrooms!

I t's true, I love a 'shroom! Eating them, growing them, spotting them at the base of a particularly magickal tree . . . mushroom pizza, obvi. Mushrooms are fun guys! Sorry.

There's something so weird and alien about mushrooms that I adore, which is probably exactly why so many folks can't quite stomach them (also because they are, I'll admit, an acquired taste). But mushrooms and their cousins are actually the least extraterrestrial thing possible! They make up a huge percentage of our ecosystems— one of the largest (and oldest) living organisms in the WORLD is a colony of honey mushrooms covering over two thousand acres in Oregon. Of course this isn't just one gigantic mushroom cap, it's actually a bunch of mushrooms sharing cells and consciousness, and similar mycelium networks cover the entire planet. Like Mercury-ruled Virgo, mushrooms are amazing communicators. They're also, as Erica already mentioned,

exemplary composters, relieving the earth of everything from dead leaves to nuclear contamination, and thriving through the whole process. Totally superheroes.

MAGICK MUSHROOM MAGNET

For this spell you just need a mushroom, either from the market or in the wild. And the spell is . . . talk to the mushroom! Tell it what's bugging you. Tell it what's holding you back. If you're in the wild, imagine your words sinking down through the mushroom, through its miles of mycelia, transforming into regenerative energy that enriches the soil. If you have a culinary mushroom that isn't in soil, move it around the areas of your body where you carry stress or anxiety, and let the mushroom act

like a magnet to attract all your negative energies. When you're done, thank the mushroom, and ask it if it has anything to tell you (reciprocation is important). Then you can be on your way, or you can prepare and eat the mushroom. Since the energy you communicated to the mushroom has been alchemized, you can consider it an antidote against further poisonous thoughts.

When mushrooms naturally sprout in a circle, the formation is known as a "faerie ring"—evidence of a faerie gathering from the night before! Form your own faerie ring by casting this spell with friends to deepen your connection.

ROOT RECIPES

What could be earthier than roots?! Humans have been eating roots for over 100,000 years, and many cultures around the world have been working magick with them as well. For our purposes we're going to stick closer to the grocery store than the botanica. Eating root vegetables is a perfectly simple way to bring the earth into your body and help it to ground. If you're a seasoned kitchen witch, you probably already have some favorite dishes incorporating ingredients like carrots and ginger and potatoes. But maybe those recipes are focused on taste alone. If you're not a kitchen witch, roots are a great place to start because you can pretty much chop up and roast any combination of these humble heroes in an oven at 400 to 425 degrees Fahrenheit for about forty-five minutes, and you will have a delicious and

nutritious plate of food. To add some intention, here are some magickal correspondences to help you take your root recipes to the next level.

BEET: Earth, Love, and Beauty; Aphrodite connection

In addition to being delicious on their own, the deep-red color of beets lends itself to making many dishes prettier and pinker (which comes as no surprise, with the Aphrodite connection). Use beets to enhance self-esteem and attract love of all kinds.

CARROT: Fire, Sex, and Creativity; Mars connection

Carrots' orange color connects them with the vibration of creativity. Cook them with a sweet glaze to help attract your muses.

GARLIC: Fire, Protection, and Health; Mars connection

We all know garlic can help keep vampires away, but did you know that the ancient Greeks left offerings of garlic at crossroads for Hecate, the goddess of witches? It's true!

GINGER: Fire and Manifesting; Mars connection

This spicy root adds a ton of flavor and manifesting powers to any dish! Chew a piece of candied ginger while casting money spells for some extra oomph.

ONION: Fire and Protection; Mars connection

They can be wild, sweet, green, red, or yellow. Who doesn't love some aromatic onion, sizzling in a pan or chopped up in a delish salsa? Think of the layers as protective psychic barriers to negativity of all kinds.

POTATO: Protection and Compassion; moon and earth connection

True shape-shifters, potatoes can be worked with in so many ways, we could talk about them all day. Mix and match potatoes with different herbs and spices to flavor a protection spell for any purpose.

RADISH: Fire and Protection; Mars connection

Next time you look at a radish, remember that its peppery taste is like a prickly layer of porcupine quills for your energy. Plus the Fraggles love them, and they are delicious pickled. (Do you notice a lot of protection vibes in this section? It makes sense that food that grows within Mother Earth would be fearless and fierce.)

SWEET POTATO: Water; Giving and Receiving Love; Venus connection

The name gives it away. Root yourself in romance with some sweet potato pie!

TURMERIC: Air and Purification; Mercury connection

Turmeric is an amazing anti-inflammatory ingredient. Use it to calm hot tempers and clear the mind.

Here are a few of my favorite quick-and-dirty root recipes.

PROTECTION POTATOES

Grab some rosemary from your pleasure garden and make these potatoes to keep you safe from hunger, limiting beliefs, and vampires!

- 1 pound small potatoes
- 2 tablespoons olive oil
- ½ teaspoon salt
- ½ teaspoon pepper
- 1 tablespoon chopped garlic
- 2 tablespoons fresh rosemary

1. Preheat the oven to 400°F.
2. Cut potatoes in halves or quarters.
3. Mix olive oil, salt, pepper, garlic, and rosemary in a large bowl. Add potatoes and toss.
4. Spread potatoes on a baking sheet, and roast in the oven for about an hour.

"CALLING THE MUSE" CARROTS

These sticky but not-too-sweet carrots get an added boost thanks to cinnamon, which helps support creative vision.

- 6 carrots, peeled and sliced ¼-inch thick
- 3 to 4 tablespoons maple syrup
- ¼ teaspoon salt
- ¼ teaspoon cinnamon

1. Put all of the ingredients in a large frying pan, add 1 cup water, and bring to a boil.

2. Reduce heat, and simmer for 20 to 30 minutes, until your carrots reach the desired tenderness. (The time may vary, depending on the freshness of your carrots and the size of your pan.) Add a little more water if too much evaporates before your carrots are cooked as you like.

3. Turn heat to high, and boil rapidly, stirring carrots frequently until all the water has evaporated and your carrots have a sticky glaze that has turned slightly brown.

NOTE: While eating, keep your mind as clear as possible and have a pen and pad of paper nearby!

VIRGO VORTEX: A SUPER-ORGANIZED, HYPER-PRACTICAL, ECO-FRIENDLY, AND CURATED-TO-ABSOLUTE-PERFECTION END-OF-SUMMER FEAST!

Okay, so far we've been pretty chill while working with all this Virgo energy. But let's be honest. Virgo energy is kind of . . . a little bit . . . sometimes . . . the opposite of chill. The nice thing about Virgos gone wild is that they are amazing at channeling their whirlwind of energy into incredible results! Whether it's organizing a closet, planning an event, or some other painstaking, perfectionism-driven task, when Virgos execute their vision, don't get in their way! They simply can't be contained. With this exercise, learn to harness this energy for the good, and never look back.

So, remember when you bought that panini press, with dreams of making perfect, melty, crunchy sandwiches, only to let it collect dust more than dinners? Or when you found that ice cream maker at a garage sale, only to realize, all too quickly, why someone was getting rid of it? Like exercise equipment, home gadgets tend to become still-life installations in people's homes. We're talking about the bread makers, air fryers, vacuum sealers, smokers, steamers, blenders, juicers, and deep fryers

bought in a moment of fantasy. A moment of "This machine will help me be a person who makes their own (fill in the blank), even though I have never been that person before." Hey, sometimes those little tricks work! But more often, I fear they end up creating teeny little spirals of shame that *literally* take up too much space in our lives. Since we're in a shame-free zone here, let's utilize some Virgo energy in a kitchen ritual to clean out your cabinets, in the best possible way.

If you do not have much Virgo in your birth chart, or don't connect easily to the idea of careful planning on multiple levels of reality using different forms of consciousness, and how all of those things relate to throwing a dinner party—you may not be able to execute this all in one go. You may have to return to this ritual year after year (as I will) and fully devote yourself to getting as close to

heaven as a Virgo with a project of this scope in their hands can. If we can eventually make it to the end, I guarantee something will have shifted in our lives in a major way. Until then, I think we can just have some fun trying.

If you *do* have strong Virgo placements? GAME ON.

LEVEL 1: Clean out your kitchen. Take out all the gadgets you never use, and put them out where you can see them. Make one last attempt at working with them by using them to make a meal! Maybe you decide to keep the gadget after all. Great! If not, donate it. *OR . . . Proceed to Level 2*

LEVEL 2: Throw a pot-luck dinner party. Have your friends also make things with their little-used gadgets. People can swap unwanted things. I'm sure one of your friends would love to make

ice cream, and maybe a friend on a gluten-free diet would love to try their hand at the zoodle-maker! So fun! You did it! You're done! *OR* . . .
Proceed to Level 3

LEVEL 3: Don't just throw ANY gadget-themed dinner party. Make it an End of Summer Harvest Feast, where everyone brings dishes they made with their gadgets, *and* you swap them, *BUT ALSO* you incorporate some acorn candles in the tablescape, form a mushroom faerie ring with your guests, and put some root vegetables on the menu. Then, STOP THERE, knowing you have successfully reached a level of Virgo excellence that many simply cannot! *OR* . . .
Proceed to Level 4

LEVEL 4: Complete levels 1 through 3, *plus* incorporate your pleasure garden herbs or flowers, and put out an extra seat for your Haus spirits, so they can join in the fun! Make it a Dark Moon Dinner, and clean out your fridge at the same time. Have a sun tea on the menu, or maybe use sun-printed place cards! Then, seriously, pat yourself on the back for hosting an incredibly intentional community-building event! Just kick back and relax. *OR...*
Proceed to Level 5

LEVEL 5: Compost your leftovers. Composting makes trash into treasure for soil. It's basically alchemy! Don't have a compost setup? I can't think of a better opportunity to start one than this most practical, down-to-earth time. Let's get some buckets and worms, bestie! No, but seriously, there are some low-lift and, dare I say, cute (and wormless) points of entry into composting, even for those of

us who are apartment-dwellers. Just Google "Composting Starter Kit," and myriad options will come up. Many towns and cities have arrangements for compost pickup if you can't use composted material in your own yard or garden.

By now you've Virgo-ed so hard, you must be exhausted! Rest assured: you've made it farther than most. I'm sure your party was perfect AND you did something nice for the earth! Now you can collapse under the weight of your gold stars. *OR...*
Proceed to Level 6

LEVEL 6: You can kill your lawn, plant a native garden, and use your new compost as fertilizer. The Native Garden movement is one of the coolest ways to align yourself with a more earth-centric existence. Perfectly green, manicured lawns are another outdated project of yesteryear. A capitalism-reinforcing status symbol among the suburban middle class, lawns actually do a lot of harm to the environment.

The types of grasses used in US lawns are not native to America, which means they need a bunch of harmful chemicals to stay alive. These end up producing carbon emissions and poisoning the waterways. Speaking of which, they are also a disaster for the water supply. Americans use over five million Olympic-size swimming pools' worth of water on their lawns EVERY YEAR! Which is especially bad, considering that parts of the country are experiencing mega-droughts, and there is more lawn grass growing in our country than food crops. Lawns are literally competing with food as our most valuable resource.

Native gardening means composting your existing lawn and replacing it with plants native to the area that support the local ecosystem. I have heard these newly created yards described as "meadow paradises." Doesn't that sound nice? Wildflowers that draw butterflies and birds! Bees and other pollinators can thrive again, despite the massive (human-caused) decline in their population. Plus, you'll be in good company! The movement is gaining tons of momentum, and a few cities and counties have already incentivized doing away with the green squares. In the Nevada desert, residents can receive cash for killing their lawns, which ended up removing two hundred million square feet of grass. Native cacti and succulents replaced it.

If you aren't ready to take that much of a plunge, try being more conscientious about the plants you grow in your garden. Do away with non-native or invasive species, even if you love the look of them. Aesthetics are important, but your garden will *feel* so much more alive that you'll know it's worth the swap.

I myself don't have a lawn, and a lot of you don't either. I bet there's some activism we can conjure up around this cause, though . . . I've started lending some financial support to Grow Native Massachusetts, an organization that educates people on the Native Garden movement and channels donations toward related gardening projects, to "build a shared vision of the world that views humans as being 'of nature,' not separate from it."

Even if you don't have a lawn yourself, you likely know someone who does. Encourage them to shift away from these relics of the 1950s! All the cool kids are doing it! Plus, the process of doing this, called sheet mulching, isn't terribly hard. Basically, you cover your lawn with biodegradable cardboard (recycling all those Amazon boxes!), and then you cover the cardboard in wood chips. After a season or so, you can grow new plants and flowers in the chips. Voilà! If you're still not convinced, do a Google image search for "Native Gardens," and I bet you will be.

So I say, if you don't have a lawn, but you make a donation or volunteer some time to the Native Garden movement, you are free to move on to Level 7 . . .

LEVEL 7: YOU WIN VIRGO SEASON!!! You've checked all the boxes, and you've crossed everything off your list. Atop your head sits a crown of magickal acorns handed down from Beyoncé herself! Pat yourself on the back for a job well done, and get busy planning for next year!!!

Okay, that's enough digging in the dirt! It's time to bring in some balance with Libra season!

WISDOM
OF W
CR

Walking the
Witch Trials:
A DIY Tour of
Salem History

Libra
Season

Softness and Justice for All

September 23–October 22

- **SYMBOL:** The Scales of Justice
- **DEITIES/PLANETS:** Venus, Uranus
- **ELEMENT:** Air
- **TAROT SUIT:** Swords
- **BODY CONNECTION:** Kidneys
- **CRYSTAL:** Rose quartz

Libra season comes floating in like the pink bubble that conveys the Good Witch Glinda to Munchkin City. Airy, delicate, and ruled by Venus, Libra is often associated with beauty, aesthetics, and sensuality. We can relish this time of rose-colored reality while the energy is effervescent and soft, but eventually we must answer Glinda's crucial question: "Are you a good witch or a bad witch?" And the judgment begins.

Libra, represented by the scales of justice, is the only sign represented by an inanimate object. There's no ram, or lion, or crab, no twins or virgins or bulls. Just an object, symbolizing an ideal. This forces us to personally identify with an abstract concept like justice, and in a perfect world, balance. All good witches strive to be balanced, and to bring their best, most centered selves to working magick. Because of this, Libra is also associated with indecision, lest the wrong choice be made and throw the system out of whack.

Seasonally, Libra begins on the Fall Equinox, the time in which days and nights are equal in length. So even though Libra energy contains sweetness and light, the darker part of the year is creeping in, and some serious ideas require our attention. For example: If the scales represent truth and fairness, does our justice system live up to that ideal? As a witch in Salem whose store is about a block away from where the Salem Witch Trials went down, I definitely have a few things to say about "good witches," "bad witches," and justice. But more on that later.

As the only sign without a heartbeat, Libra invites us to take a look at ways in which we unconsciously prioritize the nameless, faceless systems that govern our lives, our own bodies, and our needs. The ways in which we take personal responsibility for systemic failures. For instance, the way I feel guilty every time I use a plastic straw, while oil companies have spilled literally millions of gallons of oil into the ocean. Or the rhetoric arguing that millennials can't afford housing because of their latte addictions and not an outrageously inflated housing market. Of course, there are always times that we can all step up and be better humans (hopefully you're getting some ideas with this book!), but at other times it does us all a real disservice to take on blame and shame while corporations do much more harm to our world than we as individuals ever could. Capitalism has a million of these little tricks to make us hate ourselves instead of the systems of oppression that impact our lives and our planet the most.

So in this season of balance, of light and dark in equal measure, we're going to explore working with lightness and take a hard look at the idea of justice. We're going to be working with radical softness, the element of air, and the heavy stuff that weighs us down. But first we've got some decisions to make.

INDECISION DIVINATION

Librans are famous for their commitment to fairness . . . and the subsequent confusion it can breed. After all, when you're preoccupied with making the most just and harmonious choice, sometimes there are a lot of variables that need to be considered! I have several Libra placements, and making decisions can sometimes feel debilitating. Luckily, over the centuries humans have devised a lot of easy and interesting ways to help make decisions through divination.

Sometimes we need a lot of otherworldly input. The kind of information that can be gleaned only by deep meditation, a full tarot reading, or a deep dive into our birth chart. Other times, we just need to flip a coin. Heads or tails? The interesting thing about flipping a coin is that it may show us what we *really want* down deep, rather than dictate the "correct" path. Have you ever assigned one option to heads and another to tails— then, when your coin lands on heads, your immediate reaction is disappointment rather than relief? You realize you weren't actually ambivalent; you wanted the choice that tails represents. This is one way in which divination works. I mean, you can see it as the universe choosing for you, or you can see it as the universe helping you get in touch with what you actually want. This play between the conscious and unconscious forces within our mind, its own version of light and dark, is the perfect thing to explore through Libra season.

PENDULUMS

It's said that the use of pendulums, or dowsing, goes as far back as the Oracle of Delphi in Greece more than three thousand years ago. Some think

pendulums work with the higher self and intuition and provide answers through the "ideomotor phenomenon," whereby a person makes motions unconsciously in accordance with their unseen wisdom or desire. Others believe the guidance to be otherworldly in nature, coming from Spirit. I'm sure it's a combo of both! Whether you feel like the guidance received by using a pendulum comes from your own mind or from divine intervention, the simplicity of the method makes it worth a try.

In my opinion, pendulums work best with yes-or-no questions.

If you don't have a pendulum, all you need is an object (called the bob) that dangles at the end of a chain or string. Obviously, there are myriad pendulums you can purchase, but a necklace works just as well! In fact, if the necklace or pendant is meaningful to you, it may provide more accurate responses. If you decide to purchase a pendulum, clear it in some sun- or moonbeams and charge it with your energy for a few days before working with it.

1. Once you're ready to ask your question, sit at a table or other flat surface. Ground and center yourself (see Introduction).
2. Establish which motion will mean no and which will mean yes. For example, if the pendulum swings in a linear, back-and-forth motion, it will stand for yes. If it moves in a circular motion, it will mean no.
3. Drop into a light meditative state while focusing on your question.
4. Hold the end of the string or chain as still as possible in your dominant hand, and rest your elbow on the table. The bob should be an inch or two above the surface.
5. Once the pendulum is completely still, ask your question out loud or in your mind and release the bob, keeping it as still as possible.
6. After a few seconds the pendulum should start moving. Once it's in full swing, read what it's telling you! Is it what you hoped to hear?

If you want to deepen this practice, there are more complex ways of working with pendulums, using charts, grids, and spirit boards!

BIBLIOMANCY

Bibliomancy is the practice of divination through books! Specifically, closing your eyes, paging through a book, stopping randomly on a word, sentence, or passage, and deciphering the message in the context of your question. Some folks like to use the Bible or another sacred text. I say use a book that you feel connected to in some way, but don't feel like it has to be a serious choice.

For example, I'm going to use *Women Who Run with the Wolves* by Dr. Clarissa Pinkola Estés, which I would personally call a sacred text. My copy is well worn and deeply loved, so

I've already established a strong energetic connection to it. I'm going to ask if I should orient my day toward writing or if I can take a break to hang with my wife. Okay, here goes:

Via page 220 of the book, the women and the wolves they run with say: "The body, through its states of arousal, awareness and sensory experiences—such as listening to music, for instance, or hearing a loved one's voice or smelling a certain fragrance—has the ability to transport us elsewhere." Seems like a pretty clear sign to close the laptop and make space for some quality time!

The beauty of bibliomancy is that you don't have to stick to yes-or-no questions. You can keep it super general and just ask for some words of wisdom from your higher power. In fact, try doing this for a week, and see if there's a larger message within your daily divining! You can also experiment with different books to find your own sacred text.

CLOUD GAZING

Okay, and now for my personal favorite type of divination, cloud gazing! I've always been fascinated by weather and storms (for better or worse), and I have a lot of air sign placements in my chart. I'm sure we've all had the experience of looking at the shapes the clouds make in the sky, but did you know that it could be a form of divination?

Cloud gazing, or nephomancy, is part of a larger grouping of divinatory techniques called aeromancy, or air divination. Ancient folks believed that the weather revealed the divine will of gods and goddesses. Aeromancy includes several techniques for reading the sky, such as anemoscopy, divination by studying the speed, direction, and sound of the wind; ceraunoscopy (also called keraunoscopy), divination by observing thunder and lightning; and brontoscopy, divination by listening to the sound of thunder.

For me, cloud gazing is so relaxing that sometimes I don't even try to interpret the shapes. I just trust that I'll know what to do when my mind is calm after a few minutes of spacing out, watching them. It's also a great way to invite the muses! Divine inspiration has come to me quite a few times while simply looking up at the sky and watching the clouds.

SOFT POWER

The idea of radical softness came to me by way of Genderfail, a trans + nonbinary publishing platform run by Be Oakley. Inspired by artist Lora Mathis, Oakley released a zine, tote bags, and other merchandise with the slogan "Radical Softness as a Boundless Form of Resistance," and the phrase intrigued me immediately. It's an idea that invites interpretation, conversation, and translation: "To challenge the terms such as 'radical' and 'resistance' as often viewed through an ableist lens as active, as against ostensibly passive forms of softness or emotiveness," as Oakley says. It is a refusal of the ways in which our world asks us to be hard, prioritizing extroversion, aggression, and violence as a means of getting things done. Radical softness is about turning away from the world where we feel like we need to fight, and turning toward the ways in which being soft and vulnerable can be revolutionary. To see softness not as weakness, just a different form of power. As Lora Mathis writes in "Soft and Radical Realities: Exploring Radical Softness as a Weapon": "To work against a patriarchal system is to tear down the stigma which binds us and separates us. To embrace our vulnerability, our pain, our wide-range

RADICAL SOFTNESS AS A BOUNDLESS FORM OF RESISTANCE

of emotions; to recognize the power in communities of care and support; to see the strength in healing; to view others in their hurt; to hold our own pain without pushing it away; this is to know our power."

As an air sign, Libra has the "boundless" thing down pat. Air is here, there, everywhere, and nowhere. When I picture a boundless form of resistance, I imagine a force as mighty as the opposition, but with infinite ability to maneuver. "Softness" is like a secret word that makes us ponder important questions: Is a softer world a more balanced world? Is a softer world possible?

One of the ways I embrace softness is by leaning into *care*. When life gets hard, I try to make sure my people are cared for. I try to ensure that my employees feel cared for. I make sure I am practicing good self-care. I look into how I can care for my wider community through mutual aid. For me this is what "fighting" for a better world looks like.

In this context, what does softness mean to you? Is it simply a refusal of hardness, a refusal of aggression, or is it something else?

How can you feel powerful in softness?

How can you find liberation through softness?

How can we create a softer world by leading by example?

WITCH CITY JUSTICE

My shop is about five hundred feet from where the old Salem courthouse stood—and less than a mile from where the accused witches were hanged during the Salem Witch Trials. HausWitch is technically on the property owned by the evil High Sheriff George Corwin, who ordered the execution of twenty innocent people. As I write this it is July 19, the very day that Sarah Good, Elizabeth Howe, Susannah Martin, Rebecca Nurse, and Sarah Wildes were carted from that courthouse to Proctor's Ledge for execution 331 years earlier.

If they were making that trip today, after leaving the site of the courthouse on Washington Street, they would take a right turn at the *Bewitched* statue and head up Essex Street, past souvenir shops proudly displaying upside-down pentagrams and selling spells and poppets. They'd pass busy

cafés, dentist offices, tattoo shops, and even my current home on the way to the gallows. They would roll past the new-at-the-time mansion of Judge Jonathan Corwin (uncle of George), which is now a museum known as the Witch House, an ironic twist. Across the street from Judge Corwin's former dwelling now stands The Good Witch of Salem, a Barbie-pink children's store aimed at "using the gift of magick to guide children toward love and kindness in our world."

Eventually the condemned five would make it to what is now a Walgreens parking lot and climb the hill between Proctor, Pope, and Boston Streets. There George Corwin would put the rope around each one's neck and kick the stool out from under her feet.

If you're not familiar with the witch trials, I will try to catch you up. The trials are a mysterious and nuanced phenomenon, but I'll do my best.

In 1486, in Germany, an extremely sick and twisted book, *Malleus Maleficarum* (*The Hammer of Witches*), was published by two medieval incel losers. It detailed how to find, arrest, assault, and kill witches who, according to them, were of course mostly women. Women were more susceptible to influence from the devil, due to their innate wickedness and sexual desire. This kicked off centuries of brutal witch hunting in Europe, where tens of thousands of people (again, mostly women) were executed for supposedly being in league with the devil. Actually, they were just poor, old, or disabled; some were

Jewish, or considered outsiders for other reasons, or were victims of petty disputes with neighbors.

In the seventeenth century this type of misogynist witch hunt crossed the Atlantic Ocean and landed in New England. It's not surprising, since fear already permeated everyday life for the early Puritan settlers. On the edge of the wilderness, the nights were long and pitch-black. Initiating horrifying wars to steal land from the local Indigenous peoples meant violence might wait around every corner. Plagues, famine, and family feuds made Puritan New England a pretty harsh and joyless place to be. History's most famous buzzkills had come to the "new world" to escape religious persecution, but ironically would end up perpetuating their own brand of it.

The winter of 1691–92 was especially harsh, and the community was pushed to the brink. Samuel Parrish, the not-well-liked town minister, was having trouble getting his share of food and firewood from the congregation. This was causing even more strife within the tense community, but also within Parrish's own home. Then Parrish's young daughter and niece started having unexplainable fits—screaming, convulsing, shaking, crying, and basically doing the absolute most, in the way only teenage girls can.

I'm sure it was terrifying, but for us, it's pretty easy to imagine a couple of teens acting out for attention in this incredibly stifling environment: they were already in the child-bride-to-dutiful-wife pipeline and bullied because of who their patriarch was. They weren't even allowed to partake in simple pleasures like dancing! Who wouldn't have a fit?!

Eventually, more of the girls' friends started having fits (FOMO), and it was decided that witchcraft could be the only cause . . . in other words, the authorities needed a scapegoat. Early modern folks loved to blame the actual devil and all who may be in cahoots with him for their misfortunes. The men of Salem started rounding up the most vulnerable women they could find, and some truly wild accusations started flying, though actual witches *were not*. A long and complex series of "trials" started, and as winter turned to spring, shit got gnarly in ye olde Salem Towne.

There was one common denominator among the first folks arrested for supposedly being witches: they were different. Poor or hard to control in some way, they revealed the cracks in Puritanical society and they would be punished for it. But as the spring went on, more and more people, even respected ones like seventy-one-year-old Rebecca Nurse, a pillar of the community, were accused of being in league with the devil. As things spiraled out of control in Salem, the need for a scapegoat grew more intense.

By the fall of 1692, over two hundred people had been arrested, and nineteen had been hanged at Proctor's Ledge (one more was pressed to death under heavy stones on the other side of town). They even executed two dogs for being familiars!

I recently made the short journey on foot from the site of the courthouse to the gallows. I left an offering of flowers at the recently erected monument, and I asked the nineteen people memorialized there what they wanted the world to know about the trials and justice. Here's what I got:

1. Everyone was a witch, and no one was a witch. Meaning, while none of the accused were self-identified witches, many people in the community were practicing the kind of folk magick that today we would associate with witchcraft. In fact, one of the accusers, Mary Sibley (who went on to live a long life after the trials), baked a "witch cake" to try to determine who the real witches were. Mixing rye flour with urine from the afflicted girls and then making the family dog eat the cake was a standard countermagick practice among early modern people. As were carving protective symbols on your doors and stuffing everything from shoes to dead cats into the walls to block witches from entering. These practices were not condoned by the church and were considered casual sorcery. But almost everyone did them.

2. None of the eventually executed victims pleaded guilty; they all maintained their innocence and their devotion to god until the end. These were god-fearing Christians, not devil worshippers. Their religion meant so much to them that they died as martyrs, while others who pleaded guilty were allowed to live.

3. Not a single one of the accused witches was given a fair trial (by modern standards), nor were

they considered *innocent until proven guilty*. In the court that the governor of Massachusetts literally invented for these trials, claiming that someone's spirit had harmed you was allowed as evidence (specifically, spectral evidence), as was blatant hearsay. But, conveniently for the prosecutors, defense attorneys were forbidden.

Under those circumstances, what does it matter if the victims were witches or not? Anyone would lose. At the heart of the Salem Witch Trials was not just concern about what goes bump in the night, but a need for social control amounting to state-sponsored terrorism. It worked. The trials have cast a shadow centuries long.

The witch trials got our country's criminal justice system off to a pretty rocky start, but things still aren't great. We have the highest rate of incarceration in the entire world. Though our population makes up only 5 percent of the world's total, the United States accounts for 25 percent of the world's prisoners.

When I was retracing the steps of these Salem victims, I thought of another instance in which five people were sacrificed in the name of scapegoating dressed up like justice. In 1989, five Black and Latino teenagers named Korey Wise (16), Antron McCray (15), Raymond Santana (14), Kevin Richardson (14), and Yusef Salaam (15) were accused of attacking a female jogger in New York City's Central Park. Despite having nothing to do with the attack, aside from being in the same general area of the city, the boys were arrested, bullied, beaten, and lied to relentlessly until they "confessed" . . . having never spoken to attorneys. They each spent between seven and thirteen years of their young lives behind bars, before being completely exonerated in late 2002.

In this case, as in Salem 1692, the need for a scapegoat

was stronger than the need for truth and justice: New Yorkers demanded an explanation for this random act of violence, and the police gave them one. In similar circumstances, Black men and other people of color have been unfairly criminalized for centuries, partially due to groundwork laid by the US Constitution's Thirteenth Amendment. It states that it was illegal to own slaves, but someone convicted of committing a crime could be punished with involuntary servitude. Hence, the modern prison industrial complex was born. Over the next century, scapegoating Black folks for every type of crime was propped up by politicians and the white supremacy at the heart of the justice system.

Today a stunning 50 percent of incarcerated folks are people of color. Black men represent about 40 percent of the prison population, even though they make up only about 6 percent of the overall US population. Those numbers speak to rampant racial discrimination and an extremely unbalanced criminal justice system. The adoption of "mandatory minimums," or predetermined punishment for certain crimes, allowing no other factors (such as widespread systemic failures and prejudices) to be considered when handing down punishments, has led to 97 percent of criminal cases ending in plea bargains. Because now, as during the witch trials, confessing to crimes, whether or not people committed them, brings a lesser punishment. Still, the stigma of conviction will haunt those people for decades to come.

In 1692, the residents of Salem simply couldn't tolerate the idea that their harsh lives and string of misfortunes could be mainly the product of their own culture. There had to be a malevolent force behind it. And there was! It was called colonialism! The real devil in this case was white supremacy and patriarchy, same as now! In the case of the Central Park Five in 1989, the public could not tolerate the idea that the attack on the jogger was random. So the fervor and public outcry led the police to take the laziest and most racist route to "solving the case."

So let's talk about some ways that we can support victims of wrongful imprisonment and scapegoating today. Let's start with a little early modern folk magick, a reclamation of and tribute to the accused witches, and then talk about practical things we can all do to work some tangible reparative justice.

LITTLE PRICKS WITCH BOTTLE SPELL

Early modern Europeans, including Puritans, often practiced a form of witchcraft called sympathetic magick. The technology of sympathetic magick, in simplest terms, is based on this idea: I do something to an object representing a person, and it has a desired effect on that person (think of movies you've seen, in which sticking pins in a doll was meant to harm someone). Sympathetic magick was also used for protection. Carving symbols on the door, hiding shoes in the wall, and making poppets were meant to keep evil spirits and witches away from the home. Going so far as to bake urine into cakes and fill bottles with rusty nails, fingernails, and hair (and urine, Puritans *loved* working magick with urine . . .), these folks were doing witchy stuff all the time! Though officially condemned by the Puritan church because of its pagan roots, sympathetic magick was secretly all the rage for centuries. So, while I'm not going to make you work with urine, we are going to cast some sympathetic magick for our brothers and sisters

behind bars (and honestly, if you want to piss on the justice system, I'm really not going to stop you, lol).

ACCESSORIES

- 1 recycled bottle or jar with a top (Glass preferably, but use what you've got.)
- 5 pins (Straight pins, safety pins, and even hair pins will work!)
- 1 taper candle

1. Start by removing any labels from your bottle and washing it thoroughly.

2. Lay the five pins in front of you. Ground and center yourself.

3. Pick up one pin and say, "So justice can live, racial profiling must die," and place the pin in the bottle.

4. Pick up another pin and say, "So justice can be served, judicial corruption must be corrected." Into the bottle it goes.

5. For the third pin: "So justice can be compassionate, mandatory minimums must be abandoned."

6. For the fourth pin: "So justice can flourish, false evidence must perish."

7. For the fifth pin: "So justice can be measured, scapegoating must end."

8. Put the top on your container.

9. Light the candle. Imagine its flame forming a layer of care and protection around anyone you personally know in the prison system, or a particular group of imprisoned people to whom you feel a distinct connection (for me, that would be women and those imprisoned for drug-related crimes).

10. Carefully tip the candle over the bottle, and let the wax drip over the top like a seal.

When you're finished, keep your witch bottle close while you research some more practical ways of working some empathetic magick in the world.

EMPATHETIC MAGICK

THE INNOCENCE PROJECT:
Started in 1992, the Innocence Project works to exonerate wrongfully incarcerated folks and reform the legal system to prevent future injustice. In 2012 they expanded to the Innocence Network to more effectively concentrate on cases at the state and local levels. Their work focuses on using postconviction DNA evidence to overturn wrongful convictions and also to address coercive plea deals, false confessions, and delinquent defense attorneys. Consider donating under the name of one of the witch trials victims or another wrongfully imprisoned person with whom you feel a connection. The money goes toward the organization's mission and toward supporting exonerees after they are released. You can also sign petitions, volunteer, or buy merch from its online store.

THE LAST PRISONER PROJECT:
While marijuana has been legalized or decriminalized in many states, there are still a lot of folks locked up for weed-related crimes. Most are Black, and most of those making money from legal weed dispensaries are white. Organizations like the Last Prisoner Project help free those imprisoned for cannabis-related crimes and support them upon release.

WORTH RISES: The Thirteenth Amendment set up the legal use of unpaid labor as punishment, something way too close to slavery, within the prison system. Today, organizations like Worth Rises aim to close that loophole and make the prison industry more equitable. On average, US imprisoned workers make 86 cents a day (while the private prison industry makes millions off their labor). That barely covers phone calls home (which run about a dollar a minute) and commissary accounts. Speaking of, many organizations make it possible for you to donate to prisoner commissary accounts, often the only means through which these folks can get basic necessities and additional food within the prison system.

THE NATIONAL CENTER FOR TRANSGENDER EQUALITY: Trans people are much more likely to experience violence and abuse in prison than their cisgender counterparts. They are also often refused gender-affirming care and medical care, and are often subjected to longer stays in solitary confinement. The National Center for Transgender Equality uses an established network to provide publications, research, and technical assistance to local advocates fighting for trans rights throughout the criminal justice system.

BLACK MAMA'S BAIL OUT: Now known as National Bail Out, this organization began as the Black Mama's Bail Out on Mother's Day in 2017. Its massive fundraising effort on behalf of Black mothers in jail while awaiting trial[1] was originally tied to Mother's Day but has expanded in recent years. According to the group's website, "Sixty percent of people in local women's jails have not even been convicted of a crime and are awaiting trial—and 80 percent of them are parents." Bailout funds help keep families together by giving mothers back the precious time they would lose awaiting trial, which can devastate innocent people on both sides of an arrest. Like many organizations with seasonal ties, most of National Bail Out's donations come in May,

---

1   "We use the term 'Mama' to encompass all Black women and femmes that self-identify as a Mama—including cis and trans women, femmes, gender-nonconforming people, and nonbinary folks—who parent and care for their families and communities in various traditional and nontraditional ways. We are not just speaking about birth and biological mothers." See http://www.nationalbailout.org/history.

so why not help out now, during Libra season. This time of year can be especially tough on families!

So as you can see, 331 years later we still have a lot of challenges ahead in upholding the whole "freedom and justice for all" part of the US mission statement. Take a lesson from Witch City—we all might be just one false accusation away from being locked up unjustly.

Luckily, there are so many ways that anyone can help by leaning into care and working a little empathetic magick.

Once you've taken some tangible action, dismantle your Little Pricks witch bottle and recycle the elements appropriately.

Okay, witches, the scales are tipping and the days are getting shorter. It's time to dance with the dead in Scorpio season!

Scorpio Season

Truth or Scare

October 23–November 21

CORRESPONDENCES

- **SYMBOL:** The Scorpion
- **DEITIES/PLANETS:** Mars and Pluto
- **ELEMENT:** Water
- **TAROT SUIT:** Cups

- **BODY CONNECTION:** Reproductive organs
- **CRYSTAL:** Garnet and bloodstone

I'm writing this from a two-hundred-year-old cabin, in the middle of the night. The owner of the cabin, Lenore, made a point of telling me that it was built in 1796, "When George Washington was president!" as a proud grin stretched across her face. There is a prehistorically huge and loud buzzing insect in here with me. Did I ever tell you about my intense fear of bugs? There's no way to let him out because none of the windows will open. And you know how your skin gets kind of itchy when things are buggy, whether there are actual bugs on you or not? Yeah, that's totally happening. So here we are, in Scorpio season.

I've been working on this chapter for a little while now and, true to form, it's proving to be elusive and full of mystery! I feel a lot of pressure to get it right, which is intimidating, to describe the vibe of Scorpio, which makes it inherently hard to explain, even for me, a Scorpio Rising. It's like the call is coming from inside the haunted Haus (or the two-hundred-year-old cabin,

I was fully dressing up like a "fortune teller" and reading playing cards in a makeshift basement "psychic parlor" by age nine. My parents started referring to me as "morbid" at around eleven, and my thirteenth-birthday cake was in the shape of a tombstone. That's around the time I started dying my hair black, which I still do. Despite personally feeling like the softest softy on the inside, for my entire life people have described me as "intimidating." Also, I'm obsessed with secrets, but don't tell me any, because my Gemini placements love to gossip, lol. Embodying Scorpio and explaining Scorpio are two different things, so the rituals in this chapter will ask you to embody aspects of the season that can't quite be explained.

Scorpio is a water sign, corresponding to our emotional life, but unlike Cancer, this water is not a gentle tide or a day at the beach. Scorpio is about deep, dark currents full of strange creatures and sunken treasure. Over

80 percent of the earth's oceans remain unexplored, unknown darkness, with absolutely zero sunlight making it past the "midnight zone" a thousand meters below the surface. So much of working with Scorpio energy is about exploring this kind of uncharted territory, but within our own subconscious mind.

Just to be extra, Scorpio has two *intense* planetary rulerships. Traditionally it was designated as ruled by Mars only, but in modern astrology it's also ruled by Pluto. Scorpio's relationship with Mars is different from Aries's fiery, aggressive one. Scorpio's vibe with Mars is more of a cold, revenge-flavored dish. As for the correspondence with Pluto, well, as soon as astronomers found the strange, distant planet in 1930, Scorpio was reassigned. Named for the god of the underworld, Pluto, the farthest planet from the sun, is the one we know the least about. She's waaaaaay out there, and she too deals in hidden and transformative powers.

Scorpio energy is all about seeing the unseen, exposing what lies beneath, and getting nice and comfy in THE VOID. Scorpio season is a time when things are transforming all around us. Unlike Taurus, a season of growing, Scorpio is a season of dying, which is a transformation nonetheless! Embodying this cathartic energy, we're going to be grappling with ghosts and facing our fears. We're going to transmute what's no longer serving us and embrace the cycles of death and rebirth.

LET'S TALK ABOUT DEATH, BABY

The tarot card associated with Scorpio is number 13, DEATH, and it's widely known to strike fear into the hearts of those who pull it (especially in popular culture). I get it! Death's image from the popular Smith-Waite deck features a skeleton on a horse wearing black armor, waving a black flag, and trampling over its victims. All of which is very scary! But there are other subtler symbols that speak to the card's true meaning: death is not a singular event but part of a cycle. Endings are also beginnings, and wherever death goes, a rebirth is sure to follow. (Please trust me when I say that pulling the Death card never, ever means that you or anyone else is actually going to physically die.)

When you look carefully, you'll see that there is a sun on the horizon. Is it rising or setting? There's no way to tell. A white rose appears on the black flag that Death is waving, representing a blooming of the self. The horse's leg is in motion; there's a boat floating by on a body of water. Things are not static, they are moving. When it shows up in a reading, Death is

letting us know that something in our lives is no longer serving us, and it's time to let go. This is not a passive process, it's not something *happening to us* that's forcing us to shift (shout-out to the Tower). No, Death requires a sacrifice. You have to surrender something old in order to welcome in the new. Every time we die and are reborn in this way, we get closer to our authentic self, which can seem scary, but it is worth its weight in bones.

Up until modern times, death was much more present in everyday life. People died at home rather than in hospitals. Families dug their own graves and lit their own funeral fires. During wars and plagues and famines (there have been A LOT of them!) you could hardly walk down the street without seeing a dead body! Now, I'm not saying that this made death any less scary, just less mysterious. Nature's cycles of death and rebirth were more central to the lived experiences of most people.

Today, on the other hand, we are more detached from these natural cycles, and death is kept behind closed doors. People die in hospitals or nursing homes. Their bodies are brought to the morgue by a stranger in a hearse, where the corpse is prepared by another stranger, behind another closed door. We've shifted death from being a part of our everyday lives to the realm that the French philosopher Michel Foucault described as a "heterotopia."[1]

---

1   Now this is one of my favorite takeaways from grad school, so indulge me. Simply put, according to Foucault, a heterotopia is a space that "others." It is a space, physical or theoretical, that exists to contain something that would disturb or upset the normative environment. It's not good or bad, it's just different. He names cemeteries as an example. The cemetery exists to keep death away from the living. It holds space for the dead, whereas everything outside the cemetery is for the living.

Heterotopias, like death, are neutral. They aren't good like a utopia or bad like a dystopia. I have argued that in a way, Salem is a Witch-topia, or a heterotopia for witches. Throughout the rest of the world witches are feared, but in Salem, they are revered.

Only by shining a light on what's hidden can we demystify death's power over us. By shoving it to the margins, we've taken it out of context and relegated it to the realm of shadow and loss and fear.

As far as tarot goes, our fear of the Death card lies in our ego's fear of losing control. We need to remind ourselves that the only constant in life is change. The other figures on the card show us different reactions to such change, and different ways of dealing with it. The king figure, who's doing pretty well under the status quo and is therefore the most resistant to change . . . is being trampled to death. The pope, also doing okay for himself in his golden robes, stands in the way of death, praying or pleading for it to stop. The young maiden (from the Strength card) is on her knees, looking away in surrender. But in the bottom foreground there is a child, actually welcoming death with a bouquet of flowers. You may be thinking, "Is this child some sort of scary demon baby?" No, it's just an innocent kid not yet taught to fear the reaper.

If you're curious about what may need to be put to death in your own life, try this simple tarot spread. It may help illuminate where you're lost in the dark. Pull out your Death card and put it in the middle, and then pull one card for each prompt:

1. What inside of you is ready to be surrendered?
2. What inside of you is ready to be reborn?
3. What resistance (if any) may be standing in the way?

If you don't have a trusted tarot guidebook, lots of interpretation can come from simply looking deeply at the image on the card and noticing what jumps out at you. I promise, you're more intuitive than you think! Also https://biddytarot .com is a great internet resource.

PAMELA COLMAN SMITH

There have been many versions of tarot cards throughout the ages, and these days it seems like there is a deck with artwork for every possible niche. While all standard tarot decks contain the same seventy-eight cards, made up of twenty-two Major Arcana cards (like Death) and fifty-six Minor Arcana cards, the art and design of those cards can be drastically different. Perhaps the most recognizable tarot-related imagery in the Western world comes from one deck, commonly known as the Rider-Waite deck. Rider refers to the publisher, William Ryder and Son, and Waite is Arthur Waite, who commissioned the deck. But who drew the illustrations that have become almost synonymous with the tarot itself, you might ask? Her name is Pamela Colman Smith, and her hidden history deserves to be told.

Born in England in 1878, Pamela was of English and Jamaican descent. She traveled with a theater troupe early in life and bounced around between England, New York, and Jamaica for much of her life. She loved to tell stories and perform Jamaican folktales, believing that "folklore was living mythology." At age fifteen she enrolled in the Pratt Institute in Brooklyn to study drawing and painting. It was here that she learned about the concept of synesthesia, the interplay of the senses whereby one can hear colors or see music. Colman Smith taught herself to paint the visions she saw when listening to music.

A prolific writer and artist, she collaborated with prominent writers such as William Butler Yeats and Bram Stoker. A true Renaissance woman, Colman Smith also worked in costume design and stage production. In 1899 she began publishing

Intention Obsession

her own stories in addition to illustrating other people's. Over the next ten years she developed her signature illustrative style, which critics praised for its imaginativeness. Yet despite this acclaim, as a woman she often faced rejection from publishers.

This experience eventually led her down a spiritual path through the Order of the Golden Dawn, a group dedicated to alchemical understanding and occult practices. Her work began to incorporate more spiritual imagery, and she became a master at making religious and archetypal energy feel familiar to the viewer. These roads all came together in 1909 with Arthur Waite's commission for the tarot deck. Up until that time most tarot decks had illustrations only for the Major Arcana and Minor Arcana cards, which come in four suits; other cards looked more like playing cards. Colman Smith created a unique image for every single one of the seventy-eight cards, powerfully evoking the subtle energies of the cards through her keen understanding of emotion, sensuality, and symbolism.

In a letter to a friend, Colman Smith admitted that the tarot deck was a "big job for very little cash," and unfortunately it did not bring her much material success. After finishing the project she began making art for the suffragist movement and converted to Roman Catholicism. She kept writing and illustrating throughout her life, but never bridged the gap between genius and commercial success. She never married but had close female friends, whom some have speculated were her lovers. She died in 1951. In 2009, a hundred years after the Rider-Waite was published, US Games Systems released the "Smith Waite Centennial Edition" of the deck, prioritizing Colman Smith's name and using her original colorways.

PSYCHIC SECURITY SYSTEM

While we're casually processing our deepest fears, I'll tell you that besides insects, I have a lot of fear around leaving the Haus. As an introvert and indoor cat, I sometimes find that stepping out of my natural habitat can trigger deep anxieties, and the pandemic only made things worse. In fact, during the earliest days of the pandemic I wouldn't leave unless my wife was home to ensure that nothing bad would happen while I was gone.

As life has gotten back to (a new) normal, leaving the Haus more is something I've had to get used to again. One of the ways I cope is by setting a psychic security system every time I do. This little bit of threshold magick is perfect for this liminal season, and is always useful in helping me feel good about going out. Plus, I promise it's discreet enough that your neighbors will never be the wiser.

1. Right before you walk out the door to leave, turn and face the inside of your home.
2. Just for a second, imagine you're future-you, coming home later and everything is the same, safe and sound. Okay, you're good to go.
3. Once you're outside of your space, turn and face the front door.
4. Put your dominant hand on the door and close your eyes.
5. Briefly imagine a white glowing bubble of safety and protection around the entire space. If you live in a building with many homes, you can start with your space and then expand the bubble to include the entire building if you want.
6. Now, just open your eyes and go about your day! Trust that your bubble will hold everything good in and keep anything bad out.

If a bubble of protection doesn't resonate with you, here are a couple of other ideas:

CREATE AN INVISIBLE INK SIGIL SHIELD: Our ancestors used to carve and paint symbols of protection onto their homes,

and so can we! Even if we have a condo association to answer to! For this version, complete steps 1 through 4, but instead of a bubble, trace a sigil of protection with your forefinger on your front door every time you leave.

WHISPER A PROTECTION PASSWORD TO YOUR SECRET SECURITY SPHINX: In ancient mythology, sphinxes (mythical creatures with the head of a human, the body of a lion, and the wings of an eagle) were considered the protectors of portals. They guarded everything from palaces to temples and tombs. Those who wanted to pass by the sphinx had to answer her riddle correctly, and if they answered wrong, she ate them! So first, visualize your sphinx and then agree on a secret word. When you leave the Haus, again complete steps 1 through 4, and then whisper your secret word. Go about your day knowing that your sphinx has your home in her capable hands . . . or claws . . . or paws? Who knows?! It's a riddle!

NOW LET'S TALK ABOUT SEX, BAY-BEEE!

Scorpio rules the reproductive organs, after all . . . Talk about being reborn—what could be more life affirming than an orgasm?!

I won't get too into it here because I really don't need to. It's pretty simple: sometimes in magick, and I know this to be true, the secret ingredient is an orgasm. Use sex to give your intentions a little boost. Kind of like an exclamation point at the end of a sentence. A closing ceremony of sorts. By yourself or with a partner, you decide! Give yourself bonus points if you can remember to connect with your intention while climaxing!

FRESH TO DEATH
FLOWER-DRYING RITUAL

Whether you call it Halloween, Samhain, Día de los Muertos, or something else, humans all over the world have decided that the period from roughly October 31 to November 2 is about dancing with their beloved dead. Well, truthfully, *Halloween* is about costumes and candy, but the older cultural traditions it draws from are about honoring and connecting with our family and close kin who have moved on to the spirit realm.

But sometimes, our family in spirit reveals themselves in ways we wish they wouldn't. Now, I'm not talking about your grandpa's ghost knocking a picture off the wall (although that would be freaky!), I'm talking about generational patterns like addiction, guilt trips, shame spirals, neurosis, self-consciousness, hyper-vigilance, and so on. Whoa, shit just got deep, huh? Well, that's Scorpio season for ya! After all, we are dealing in hard truths and looking in dark mirrors. For this ritual we're going to respectfully release some of the power these

inherited patterns have in our lives. We're going to call on the energy of that little flower child on the Death card and welcome the spirit of transformation, even if it is dressed like a skeleton.

Using flowers in funerary rights has been a part of human culture for tens of thousands of years, so if it ain't broke, don't fix it—but maybe remix it? Instead of leaving flowers for the dead, we're going to use intention to give them, and in turn ourselves, a new life.

As you'll see, drying flowers is an incredibly simple process, but figuring out what types of patterns and trauma you'd like to transmute isn't, so take it slow and be gentle with yourself. Since you'll perform this ritual as close to Halloween as possible, you may want to start contemplating a few days to a week ahead of time. This is some intense Scorpio realness and may be a painful process, so as with any shadow work you do, go only as deep as you feel safe going.

If you need some lighthearted inspiration, look up "unserious generational curses" on TikTok. These definitely qualify!
Do this ritual anytime from October 30 to November 2.

ACCESSORIES

- A pinch of salt
- 1 white or beeswax candle
- Two 13-inch lengths of twine
- A bouquet of freshly bloomed flowers with excess foliage removed (and thrown in your compost! Wink, wink, Virgos!)

1. Sprinkle a few grains of salt in a circle around you for protection. Ask for the guidance and protection of your ancestors.

2. Light the candle.

3. Lay out one length of twine horizontally in front of you.

4. Close your eyes and reflect on the inherited patterns you'd like to transform. Anything from your grandfather's hot temper to deeper, more abstract patterning, like holding a scarcity mindset or generational privilege.

5. Now assign a flower or two to represent each inheritance. You don't have to assign something to every single flower, especially if the bouquet is large. You can even just work with a single flower if you want.

6. Hold each flower and meditate for a few moments on the inheritance you've assigned to it. Then set the flower down in front of you, with the bloom pointed toward you and its stem on the twine. Repeat with all the flowers.

7. Bunch the flowers together, wrap the twine around the stems seven times, and tie

a tight bow or knot. Flip the bouquet and hold it upside-down.

8. Thank the flowers, and acknowledge your ancestors for the whole and complex people that they were in their lives on earth. When we heal our own patterns, we heal theirs as well.

9. Use the other length of twine to hang the bouquet upside-down in a cool, dark place where it won't be in direct sunlight until the end of Scorpio season.

10. On November 21, or as close to it as possible, carefully display your dried bouquet on your altar or somewhere meaningful to remind you of the transformative healing work you've done! Your flowers are reborn!

PLUTO IN SCORPIO: REVENGE OF THE MILLENNIALS!

As long as we're out here on Pluto, talking about generational patterns and ancestral healing, we should talk about why these conversations are coming up more and more in our lives as well as in popular culture and social media. The reason: millennials are grown-ups now.

It takes from twelve to twenty-four years for Pluto to move through a single zodiac sign, roughly the time frame that defines a generation. Millennials are (largely) the Pluto in Scorpio generation.2 Anyone born between November 6, 1983, and November 10, 1994, has this placement. Based on what we already know about Scorpio (has a kink about doing shadow work, not afraid of the dark, deep emotional capacity) and Pluto (loves to reveal what's hidden and take trips to the underworld), we can understand some of what is driving this societal awakening around things like mental health, understanding trauma, and breaking toxic cycles. Forced to exist in the fallout from the world built for them by previous generations, millennials have navigated crisis after crisis, and we've had to do a lot of soul-searching to figure out how to thrive in a broken world, while laying some groundwork for a new one.

But before we can move forward, we have to look back,

---

2   Born in 1982, I am technically one of the very eldest of millennials, and so my Pluto is in Libra. These things are not always precise! That's okay!

and Pluto in Scorpio folks are out here every day trying to figure out where it all went wrong. By diving deep into the complex matrices of power (capitalism, white supremacy, colonialism, and misogyny) and calling them out for what they are, millennials are exposing the lies our world is built on. (Gen Z, the Pluto in Sagittarius generation, has definitely picked up this torch and is running with it in a way I really appreciate.) This work is important for us all, and it can start with your family tree and extend to the whole human race through ancestral healing.

Doing reparative ancestor work can be tough but incredibly rewarding. Not only can we cultivate empathy and compassion for those in our lineages who were victims of exploitative systems, but we can also address the ways in which some of our ancestors perpetrated and upheld toxic power structures (like slavery, racism, religious trauma, discrimination, anti-Semitism, and homophobia) and take responsibility for healing those legacies and engaging in reparative justice. More and more research proves that generational trauma lives in our bodies, meaning those hungry familial ghosts literally live in our blood and bones.

For example, ovaries develop in utero with all their eggs ready to go. That means that for those of us with ovaries, half of our DNA already existed and experienced living in our grandmothers' wombs. Since trauma is stored in the body, any stresses that our mothers or grandmothers experienced while pregnant are still imprinted on us at this very moment. Now, I don't know all of the specifics, but based on what I do know about my mother, her family, and the wider experience of most women under patriarchy, I can go ahead and assume that there is some pretty dicey stuff going on in my epigenetic pathways.

My maternal grandmother died long before I was born. Her absence loomed large over my own childhood because of the traumatic impact her death had on my mother. However, I realized in my thirties that I knew more about her ghost than who she was when she was alive. So I decided to try to cultivate a relationship with her in spirit.

First, I stopped referring to her as "my mom's mom who died before I was born" and started referring to her as Grandma Barbara. Just that little shift was enough for her to start making her energetic presence more, well, present. In the years since, I have patched together as much information as I can, with the limited ability I have to be in contact with that side of my family. She was born on April 28, which happens to be the day I signed the lease for my store. I know she baked a mean cinnamon roll, and so I started to burn cinnamon incense in her honor. She had a rebellious spirit and a great sense of humor. She loved Billie Holiday, but her favorite song was "Crazy Mama" by J. J. Cale, an uncomfortable bit of foreshadowing for me, lol. She grew up in scarcity, which led to her being obsessively rigid at times, something I understand on a deep level. She gave up her job as a retail buyer when she settled down and started raising her five children. She hated being economically dependent on my grandfather for survival, so she was insistent that my mother and aunt take education and career seriously, so they wouldn't be in that position themselves. This was one thing that my mother actually did repeat to me early and often, and I definitely inherited a fierce independent streak as a result.

Since cultivating this relationship with Grandma

Barbara, my successes are her successes too. And not just because I can really feel her supportive presence quite strongly most of the time now, but also because I'm living the kind of independent, fulfilling, and liberating existence that many women of her generation could only dream about. I don't have to subject myself to the kind of self-sacrifice that many of our female ancestors did. I have so many more choices to choose and paths to walk down, and it's just really nice to think about Barbara, and all the women in my family line, getting to share in that experience with me.

WHAT DOES THE FUTURE NEED FROM US?

Inviting what Daniel Foor, author of *Ancestral Medicine: Rituals for Personal and Familial Healing*, would call "well ancestors" into our lives can be really rewarding personally, but it can also help us heal the legacies of intergenerational pain. For now I just want to reference his framework for identifying different types of ancestors and some ways of doing healing work with each:

FAMILY ANCESTORS

These ancestors are your nearest and dearest departed. Your biological family and/or adoptive and chosen family. These are the people you were surrounded by in life, who were very present and familiar. You may already have rituals of remembrance that you perform for these folks, like leaving flowers at a gravesite or wearing a piece of jewelry you inherited from them. If not, try to cultivate a simple practice like lighting a candle on their birthday or a significant anniversary or leaving an offering on your altar.

Every year on my dad's birthday I leave an offering of black coffee, something he loved in life, next to a photo of him and red flowers.

REMEMBERED DEAD

Family ancestors are also considered Remembered Dead, but this category extends to folks on your family tree going back a couple of generations who are unknown to you, but might be remembered by older living relatives. People whose names we know and can possibly learn more about with a little research. To my surprise, there was actually a lot of information about my people on the internet via immigration and census documents, a lot of which list their birthdays so I can (and do!) look up birth charts for many of them. I find that simply making an effort to know more creates a connection.

OLDER ANCESTORS AND THE COLLECTIVE DEAD

Zooming out further, we can try to connect with ancestors whose names are unknown to us and are usually grouped together as a sort of collective in our consciousness. I don't know much about mine except that they were mostly German farm folk, and a few Irish, who eventually made their way over to Milwaukee, Wisconsin (with a last name like Feldmann, it wasn't hard to figure that out, even without Ancestry.com). I do sense them as a warm, supportive presence in my life, but through that connection I can also sense a lot of scarcity in my family line, going back for many generations. Cultivating an abundance mindset has been an important exercise for me personally, but also in healing some of the trauma that my ancestors experienced going back generations. This grouping of ancestors can go back anywhere from five hundred to ten thousand years.

ANCESTORS OF PLACE

Another way to learn more about ancestors is through an exploration of the places they lived. I may not know much about my lineage past my great-great-grandparents, but I can dig deeper into the immigrant experience of settling in Wisconsin in the mid-1800s to learn a little more. Going back further, I can look into the history and folk traditions of rural Germany to get a sense of their culture. Even the geography itself can tell you a lot!

AFFINITY ANCESTORS

Affinity ancestors are those not linked to you through bloodlines or geography. Foor puts these into four categories: teachers and mentors, cultural heroes, ancestors of spiritual tradition, and ancestors of vocation. If you've ever felt a particular connection to a historical figure, such as a saint or a political leader, these are your affinity ancestors. This is the most abstract category, which leaves room for lots of creativity. For me, the twelfth-century German mystic Hildegard of Bingen is one of my most important affinity ancestors. Ever since first reading about her trailblazing ways as a feminist leader WAY ahead of her time, and her unabashed use of psychic visioning in her work, I have been a devoted disciple of hers. Since this prolific writer and visual artist also composed over seventy-seven hymns (many available through contemporary recordings), I can honor her by engaging with any of the arts she was involved in.

This category of ancestors can also include pop-culture characters. I firmly consider the witches from the movie *The Craft* and Arya Stark my affinity ancestors.

I love working with different types of ancestors because the process often calls attention to people or ideas that I have been mysteriously drawn to without totally knowing why. Scorpio season is prime time for reckoning with these types of enigmas.

ACTIVIST ANCESTORS
This idea comes from Sarah Lyons's book *Revolutionary Witchcraft*. These ancestors are folks who were killed for supporting a cause or because of a particular identity or othering. They are somewhat like martyrs, but not necessarily within a religious context. For LGBTQIA+ folks, the trans women of color whom I mentioned in Gemini season, who rioted at Stonewall and

fought for queer liberation, would fall into this category. Or more abstractly, perhaps, all closeted folks who had to keep part of themselves secret for their entire lives. How can we show up for them now? How can we honor their sacrifices by *intentionally* enjoying the freedoms their hard-fought battles have provided us? How can we soothe some of the wounding these ancestors endured by ensuring their losses were not in vain?

Hopefully this quick rundown can get your wheels turning about different ways of honoring your ancestors, as well as looking into your lineages for opportunities for healing and reparative work. We can ask "What does the future need from us?" and discover how this kind of looking back is essential to moving forward.

REBIRTH BATH

Now that we've walked ourselves through the Valley of the Shadow of Death, it's time for a nice bath, don't you think? Watery Scorpio season is the perfect time to incorporate some ritual bath magick. Think of your bathtub as a cauldron and the water as a potion. This can absolutely be adapted for the shower or as a hand- or footbath if you don't have a tub!

My parents used to say, "You can start your day over at any time." Meaning that if you were having a shitty day, maybe there was a way to consciously stop and pivot. Sort of like when something electronic isn't working, so you turn it off and then on again to reset it. For my fortieth birthday, I wondered if I couldn't start my *life* over at any time too.

I was lucky enough to be in a lush ayurvedic spa; for a fortieth-birthday present, my wife had arranged a custom medicinal bath with different blends of flowers and herbs, during the exact hour I was born, forty years earlier. I set an intention to clear away what was no longer serving me from the first half of my life. Even knowing that some things are deeply rooted and won't just dissolve in a fancy bath, I still set that intention. So, whether or not it actually cleared away all of my trauma (spoiler: it didn't!), it still held a lot of symbolic meaning. Submerging myself in flower water and emerging in a tropical paradise felt like the right kind of reset for my next forty years.

Do this Rebirth Bath ritual on the new moon in Scorpio. If rebirthing sounds too intense, go with themes of reinvention, reclaiming, or new beginnings.

Get creative about what you add to the bath. Start with flowers and herbs, but don't stop there!

Add some of these:

- Clean and sanitized coins to welcome in abundance

- Rose petals for increasing love
- Salt for boundaries
- Water-soluble crystals for grounding
- Seashells for emotional flow
- Bubbles for lightness
- Moonwater for growing intuition

- Sun tea for radiance
- Anything else that symbolizes what you want to soak up for your new beginning

While you're in the bath, do some scrying! Turn off the lights, light a candle, unfocus your eyes, and read your reflection in the water. Ask it what new beginning is on the horizon.

If you can, fully and intentionally submerge yourself at least once.

Now that we're learning to see in the dark, it's time to head toward the long nights and festive lights of Sagittarius season!

Sagittarius Season

Bright Lights and Dark Nights

November 22–December 21

- **SYMBOL:** The Archer
- **DEITY/PLANET:** Jupiter
- **ELEMENT:** Fire

- **TAROT SUIT:** Wands
- **BODY CONNECTION:** Legs
- **CRYSTAL:** Garnet

Sagittarius season is all about calling your shot, taking aim, and hitting your mark. Symbolized by the archer, a half-human, half-horse mythological being known as a centaur holding a bow and arrow, this is the season of go, go, go. Maybe you're the archer, but maybe you're the arrow? At different points over the course of this frenetic season, you'll probably feel like both. Ruled by Jupiter, Sagittarius comes with some major "go big or go home" vibes. But I say, why choose when you can go big AND go home?

In true Sagittarian form, this month we're *doing* A LOT. This bold and energetic sign is always on the move, looking for the next big adventure. But for those of us in the Northern Hemisphere it's a season for going inside, getting cozy, and celebrating with family and friends. So how can we honor extroverted Sagittarius energy while staying warm in the comfort of our own home?

By working with the element associated with Sagittarius: fire!

Throughout human history, a sense of community has revolved around fire. For me the thought of our early human ancestors conjures up an image of a handful of folks huddled around a fire, cooking food, warming themselves, and staving off predators. Even as civilizations evolved over the centuries and

different groups scattered all over the globe, one thing remained true: no matter how nice your living room is, people will gather around the cookfire (aka the kitchen) at parties.

And why shouldn't we turn our attention to what our ancestors did while they were at home? We certainly have enough information about what they did *outside* the home. Domestic life has long been seen as secondary in importance to the more male-dominated world of war and battles and crusades and capers. Whatever the other half of the population was doing at home (keeping everyone alive, birthing children, tending to livestock, gathering food, planting gardens, mixing medicine, and of course keeping the home fires burning) was apparently considered boooooorrrrrinnnngggg to everyone keeping track of human history for the last few thousands of years. But not to us!

This chapter is majorly inspired by a course I took with herbalist, witch, and true domestic goddexx Liz Migliorelli. Offered through her business, Sister Spinster, "Tending the Hearth" was like stepping back in time to appreciate the importance of the hearth for our ancestors as a site of community, where folktales were told, hymns were sung, and the cauldron was hung. Lessons on European folk traditions provided jumping-off points for imagining a world in which the cold season wasn't just a time to tolerate or get through, but a time to celebrate the magick of life inside. The idea really hit home for me, a former mortal enemy of the late autumn and winter months. I realized there is so much magick in hearth worship, and it was up to me to figure out how to work with it.

THE FIRST FLAME

Everyone remembers their first love, but what about your first crush on an ancient deity? At first the goddess Hestia and I didn't get off to a great start. By my senior year in high school I was a burnt-out former "gifted" student, white-knuckling it toward graduation. I decided to take a Greek and Roman mythology class but felt overwhelmed early on (truly, if you can keep all of those myths straight, I tip my laurel-wreath crown to you). Anyway, by the time the first quiz rolled around, I completely bombed it, but I distinctly remember being asked who the goddess of hearth and home was and thinking that was the most useless information anyone could possibly ask for. I even had one of those *When am I ever going to need this information in real life?!* tantrums with my parents. Twenty years later, as HausWitch was starting to come together, our paths crossed again. I started to see Hestia as a guide for my new business dedicated to the healing powers of the home. An old foe became a treasured friend. Now I have a whole business of which she is the patron deity, and I am hopelessly devoted to her. We even constructed a fireplace facade named for her in the shop, as a shrine.

So our other inspiration for this chapter will be an ode to Hestia and a reclaiming of the domestic sphere as a place of power and community. Typically relegated to the undervalued category of "women's work," Hestia is not depicted in statues or paintings. When there are representations of her, it is usually her Roman incarnation Vesta, of "Vestal Virgins" fame. And while Hestia refused offers of marriage from Apollo and Poseidon, we should still think of her "virginity" in the Virgo sense, not the purity-culture sense. In most cases, she is represented simply and elegantly by a flame.

After she refused to give up her independence, Zeus charged Hestia with watching over the home. Her main concern was the hearth fire. Not just in individual homes, but also the sacred fires at the center of each town and village. Offerings were made to her first and foremost during ritual feasts, and in turn she would keep the community flame burning.

Lately Hestia has been having a resurgence. The feminist waves of the past century or so have shifted the home front back into the spotlight. Contemporary culture is obsessed with the home space and cooking, crafting, and organizing; we're recentering the home as a site of meaning-making in a way that our patriarchy-infused culture has never before appreciated.

Fiery Sagittarius season is the perfect time to show Hestia some love and appreciation. The days are getting colder, the nights are getting longer; I can't think of a better time to devote ourselves to a little Hestia worship. Don't worry, you won't need a fireplace since over the past few hundred years our cookfires have become stovetops and ovens, and our cauldrons have become air fryers . . . nowadays it's all about kitchen witchin'.

LIGHT THE NIGHT

What better way to honor our favorite domestic fire goddess than by creating some celebratory candles? This was one of the first projects I took on during my hearth-appreciation journey, and for a candle lover it is honestly so satisfying. When you consider candles in human history, it's astonishing how central they were to bringing light to dark spaces for thousands of years. For the past three thousand years people have made candles out of everything from tallow to whale fat. For our candles we'll stick to beeswax since it's readily accessible and easy to work with.

FUN FACT: One of the first historical records of people using candles describes the early Greeks putting them on cakes dedicated to another mythological archer, Artemis, the goddess of the hunt. A sort of ancient proto-birthday cake!

ROLLED BEESWAX

If you're not up for boiling or toiling, rolled beeswax candles are as simple as it gets. All you need are some beeswax sheets and some wicks!

ACCESSORIES
- Beeswax sheets (available at many craft stores and online)
- Wicks
- A pin
- Dried herbs (optional)
- Flour glue (optional; add 1 part flour to 2 parts water, mix until smooth, and then microwave in 30-second intervals until the consistency of thick soup. Stir between each interval.)

1. Roll the beeswax tightly around a wick. Really, that's it for starting the basic version! Or you can take this opportunity to get creative about infusing the candle with your intentions. Here are some ideas.

a. Before you roll the wax sheet, use a pin to inscribe some magick words or a sigil into it. If you plan on gifting the candle, you can write a secret, supportive message to the recipient!

b. If you'd like to include herbs, roll the sheet about halfway, so the basic shape of the candle is set. Then add some of your flour glue to the bottom of the sheet. Sprinkle your dried herbs on the glue, and gently pat them down.

c. Continue rolling tightly, adding adhesive and herbs as you go.

2. Once the candle is fully rolled, press the seam tightly.

3. Stand it up straight, and press the bottom down so that it creates a flat edge.

4. Place the candle in a fireproof candleholder and light! If you used dried herbs, make sure your container can catch any stray pieces that may fall off while burning!

SIMMER SPELL

Now, if you really want to feel like a proper kitchen witch standing over a bubbling cauldron, have I got a simple spell for you! This one may require a quick trip to the grocery store, but once you've collected your ingredients, all you'll need is a pot, a stove, and water! This is an extremely easy way to infuse your home with magick and scent.

Intention Obsession

ACCESSORIES

- 10 orange slices for joy
- 10 to 12 whole cloves to welcome in abundance
- 8 to 10 juniper berries for protection
- 6 to 8 allspice berries for courage
- 12 to 16 dried cranberries for rejuvenation
- 1 long or 3 short eucalyptus sprigs for positivity
- 1 cinnamon stick to ensure success
- 1 or more bay leaves for intention setting

1. Fill a large pot about ¾ full with water, and bring to a boil.

2. Once the water is boiling, add all the ingredients except the bay leaves.

3. Think of an intention for the season, and write it on a bay leaf with a Sharpie.

4. Hold the bay leaf in your hand, and meditate on your intention for a few moments. Then drop the leaf into the pot. Repeat with more bay leaves if you want, or if you're simmering with a friend they can set their own intention!

5. Let the steam fill your home, and know that your intention is wafting out into the world along with it.

6. Continue boiling the mixture for as long as you want. Keep adding water to the pot as needed.

7. Once you're done, strain the ingredients, pop them into a jar, and refrigerate to use again in the coming days!

COZY CLOVES POMANDERS

And now for the lowest-lift option for bringing some seasonal scents into your space: some simple pomanders. They were used in the Middle Ages to prevent illness and clear the air of plague. Think of them as air fresheners that are like airborne vitamin C!

ACCESSORIES
- A bunch of whole oranges
- A bunch of whole cloves
- A nail

Making a pomander is as easy as sticking cloves into an orange in a design of your choosing. Circular patterns work best—think of rings around a planet (like Jupiter!), but it could also be great to incorporate some intention with a symbol or sigil. Use the nail to help poke holes if you want; cloves can feel a little prickly on the fingers. That's it! Put some pomanders in a bowl as a centerpiece, or hang them individually, using wire or ribbon.

SUN-AND-SPICE SOLSTICE GARLAND

Another way to subtly scent your space for the season is with a simple orange-and-cinnamon garland, which can also double as decoration! Not only are oranges traditionally associated with joy, but they also invoke something that's in short supply this time of year: the sun. The seasonal blend of cinnamon brings in the spicy scent of success, and rosemary provides protection.

ACCESSORIES
- Orange slices, ¼ inch thick
- Needle
- A few feet of twine (The length will determine how long your garland is.)
- Cinnamon sticks
- Rosemary sprigs

1. Start by dehydrating the orange slices. Lay them in a single layer on a cookie sheet, and bake for 3 to 5 hours at 170 to 200°F. While baking, flip the citrus every so often, and if the slices start to burn, turn the oven down. Let cool.

2. Thread your needle with the twine, and tie the other end to something to secure it, so the twine won't get tangled as you work.

3. Bundle one rosemary sprig and one cinnamon stick together. Tie a simple knot around the bundle to keep it in place. Create bundles from all of the cinnamon sticks and rosemary sprigs.

4. Use the needle to poke a hole through one side of a citrus slice and out the other side. Tie a knot at the end to secure.

5. Now attach a cinnamon-rosemary bundle by guiding the needle through the loop holding the bundle together.
6. Now add another citrus slice.
7. Alternate bundles and citrus slices until you use them all!
8. Hang in a window to ward off the worst of winter's impending chill!

WHAT IS BREAD MAY NEVER DIE: BAKE FOR THE ANCESTORS!

One of the ways that I deepened my intentional wintering journey was by baking bread. I had never made it from scratch before, but it turns out to be incredibly easy. Of course you can complicate and fancify, but if you just need something to dip in your stew or enjoy with a little butter or jam, you'd be surprised how easily you can make that happen.

In some ways, society itself happened because of bread. It led to the domestication of wheat and other grains, which led to people organizing themselves into towns and eventually cities and nations. As people branched out, parallel grain-centric cultures were coalescing in Asia with rice and the so-called Americas with maize. Today there is a grain-based staple food in just about every culture on earth.

After I made a very simple white loaf a few times, I started thinking about my own ancestral bread traditions. There are a lot of different types of bread made in northwestern Europe, so I decided to stick a little closer to home and make cinnamon rolls like my grandma Barbara did. I loved being able to connect with her in an active, hands-on way that tapped into some deep primordial (and delicious!) energy. So if you're still looking for ways to connect with ancestral lineages, consider doing it with bread! If working within your own culture leaves you uninspired, or if you aren't sure you've got what it takes to do the ancestors justice, you can try this recipe that our common ancestors made in caves over five thousand years ago! It's very simple, and because we're working with prehistoric tech, you make it in a frying pan rather than an oven!

Now, if you, like me, are one of the few who did not become expert sourdough bakers during the early days of the pandemic, you'll need to buy or create a sourdough starter for this recipe. It's not hard at all, but it takes a week or so. If you start it at the beginning of Sag season, it should be ready to use in time for the Winter Solstice! Alternatively you could foster community by asking your friends if they have a little starter you can borrow. That's what I did. THANKS, MAGGIE![1]

---

1   If you absolutely can't get your hands on sourdough starter, using ¼ teaspoon of instant yeast can give you similar results, but the delicious "sour" flavor won't be as strong. Just add an extra 50 grams (roughly ½ cup) of flour and an extra 50 grams (roughly ¼ cup) of water to account for the lack of starter. Thank you to my friend and bread-genius Anthony for helping me adapt the recipe!

CAVE BREAD

I love drizzling these loaves with honey or something else sweet like jam. Hummus or other savory dips pair deliciously as well. Offering a variety of toppings on the side feels very aligned with adventurous Sagittarius season!

This recipe comes from bread expert Hendrik Kleinwächter and his website, https://www.the-bread-code.io.

- 4 cups (500 grams) whole flour (rye, einkorn, or emmer)
- 1¾ cups (400 grams) water
- ½ cup (100 grams) sourdough starter
- 1½ teaspoons (10 grams) salt
- Oil or butter (optional)

1. If possible, weigh the dry ingredients with a scale rather than using measuring cups. I learned this lesson when my first batch of cave bread came out more like cave pancakes (still delicious, btw) because my flour measurement was off. (If you don't have a scale, just pay extra attention to getting the consistency of the dough right before the rising process starts.)

2. Measure and mix the flour, water, sourdough starter, and salt together until the dough has the consistency of Play-Doh. No need to knead; just thoroughly blend the ingredients.

3. Place the dough in a large bowl and cover it with a cloth. Let the dough sit for about ten hours, until it roughly doubles in size. Depending on the temperature of your house, the rise could be faster or slower. Size is the best way to determine when the dough is ready.

4. Divide your dough into four equal pieces.

5. Gently flatten and round each piece of dough, until it is roughly the size and shape of a hamburger bun. Use some oil on your hands if the dough feels too sticky to work with.

Each "loaf" should be around ⅓ inch in height.

6. Let the loaves rest while you preheat a frying pan or skillet to medium heat. Optionally, add a bit of oil or butter to the pan.

7. Add one loaf to the pan. Flip it every two minutes to make sure it doesn't burn, but rather browns nicely on each side.

8. Cooking times will vary, but after about ten minutes one loaf of cave bread should be done! Repeat the cooking process for each loaf.

SOLSTICE SOIREE: TOAST YOUR FRIENDS "AWARDS"

Sagittarius season is pretty legendary for its celebrations. Between harvest festivals, Yule, and company holiday parties, the end of November and most of December can feel like a social whirlwind. So don't worry, this gathering won't have you making a huge meal for a million people (unless you want to!), but it will leave you bursting with chosen-family cheer.

One thing sorely overlooked in our society is the importance of community. The concept of "rugged individualism," used to prop up capitalism, has downplayed the advantages of having a network of people with whom you are connected in myriad beneficial ways. The saying "It takes a village to raise a child" comes to mind. And yet, there are many single parents

and nuclear families shouldering the brunt of raising children in the US these days.

During colder months community is even more important than usual. Our ancestors needed to cooperate and collaborate in order to survive fall and winter. And not just in practical ways—social connections were bolstered by fireside storytelling, feasts, and festivals.

So why not take this opportunity to honor your community?! For this ritual you can host a little party to shine a light on your nearest and dearest. Think of it as an opposite-of-a-roast toast, a Secret Santa–style exchange where people bring compliments instead of gifts. You can even make up some "Secret Superpower" awards like "best meme sender" or "most likely to serve lewks." Sometimes the best gift you can give someone is the gift of being truly seen.

If you're more of a solo witch, try asking your tarot cards what your own superpowers are. Or ask your spirit guides!

SET THE STAGE

Luckily you've already been making candles and garlands that will be the perfect celebration decorations! You can show off your new bread-baking skills and have a fresh simmer pot boiling on the stove. Ask your friends to add their own bay-leaf intentions to the pot when they arrive. Now all you need is a glass of something sparkling to raise for each round of toasting, and a killer playlist!

THREE OF CUPS PUNCH!

The Three of Cups is one of my favorite tarot cards. The image in the Smith-Waite deck shows three people toasting one another joyfully. The card stands for friendship, community, and celebration. I often have it out near the treat table or bar at parties.

This delicious concoction can be made with alcohol, or not! Ginger beer gives it a warm kick, perfect for Sagittarius season, while the pomegranate juice is flirty and tart. Curate a few of the garnishes to cast a secret spell, or go all in and use everything! Either way, get ready to giggle!

- 2 bottles sparkling wine (For the mocktail version, use club soda.)
- 1 cup ginger beer
- 1 cup pomegranate juice
- ¼ cup sugar (optional)
- 1 cup any combination of these garnishes: thinly sliced oranges, pomegranate arils, fresh mint, cinnamon sticks, or star anise
- Ice

1. Pour the sparkling wine or club soda into a large bowl or pitcher.
2. Add the ginger beer.
3. Add the pomegranate juice.
4. Taste and add sugar if desired.
5. Add the garnishes.
6. Stir three times clockwise.
7. Right before serving, add the ice.

PARTY PLAYLIST

Ever wonder why witches are often depicted dancing around their ceremonial fires? Because dancing is super fun, duh! But also dancing is very powerful embodied magick. Letting music move you is a sort of light trance that connects you to the rhythm of life. It gets you out of your head, which (even though I don't know you personally) I'm sure you need to remind yourself to do from time to time. It's also intense energy-clearing magick. When I need to move some energy or shake off a bad day, nothing works better than dancing. Sure, I could exercise (and I will, tomorrow, I swear!), and I'm sure for many of you that serves a similar purpose, but dancing is a little different. It can clear your space too. In fact, people who visit the shop are often surprised to learn that we rarely burn herbs to clear, but boy do we do a lot of dancing.

Same goes at home. When I feel like I need to move some energy out, I crack a window or two and intentionally move through my space, imagining my Elaine Benes–like movements (no one says you have to be a "good" dancer!) stirring up the energy all around me, giving each room some movement of its own. Anything that doesn't belong can shimmy itself right out the window.

In the same way that the dark moon phase is the perfect time to clear out your fridge, these dark days are perfect for clearing your body and your space to welcome back the light. Plus, you're already having a party! Sagittarians are the official movers and shakers of the zodiac, so a little dance break seems like it should be a required ritual. If you need a little more convincing, check out this list of Sagittarius musicians and think of the epic playlist you could create from their work! Or scan this QR code to check out the one I made for you:

Miley Cyrus	Montell Jordan
Natasha Bedingfield	Jay-Z
	Nicki Minaj
Tina Turner	Sinéad
Jimi Hendrix	O'Connor
Twista	Imogen Heap
Chamillionaire	Mos Def
Steve Aoki	Taylor Swift
Billy Idol	Billie Eilish
Janelle Monáe	Christina
Britney Spears	Aguilera
Nelly Furtado	DMX

You could also curate a theme song for each friend as part of the toast. Or incorporate songs about Sagittarius's favorite things: adventure, travel, Jupiter, fire, chaos! So, whether you and your coven of cackling witches are down to clown or you're a solo centaur this season, dancing in the dark is the perfect way to spend the shortest day!

All right, my centaur superstars! This party is just getting started! It's time to climb to new heights in Capricorn season!

Capricorn
Season

Get It Together!

December 22–January 19

CORRESPONDENCES

- **SYMBOL:** The Sea Goat
- **DEITY/PLANET:** Saturn
- **ELEMENT:** Earth

- **TAROT SUIT:** Pentacles
- **BODY CONNECTION:** Bones
- **CRYSTAL:** Obsidian

Discipline, maturity, structure, determination . . . These are just a few of the super serious key words that come up when you research Capricorn vibes. Responsible, reliable, productive, stable, the list goes on and on. But then why is the mascot of this season something as silly as a sea goat? What even is a sea goat?! Maybe the ancient folks that created these mythical cosmic connections knew Capricorn needed to lighten up a bit!

But I kid! I mean, arguably one of the biggest parties of the year happens during Capricorn season, the festive and sometimes debaucherous New Year's Eve. But we all know what's next, the solemn sobering up that comes with January 1. When you think about it, what could be more on-brand for Capricorn than the idea of resolutions? Setting this type of intention requires that you tap into the very traits I just listed! Gym memberships skyrocket as people try to apply discipline and consistency to their fitness routines. Budgets are made, closets are cleaned out, and bad habits are dropped with a little help from determination and responsibility. While being extremely pragmatic, it's also pretty magickal when you think about it. The clock strikes midnight, and we believe we can be transformed!

Which brings me back to the fantastical sea goat. Some believe this curious creature comes from the god Pan, a goat-legged man who jumped into the ocean to escape the monster Typhon. Others think the association originated with the Babylonian god Ea and the goats sacrificed in his honor around this time of year. Either way, we're talking about a being that can traverse the highest mountaintops and dive deep beneath the sea. When it comes to taking the long view, thinking methodically, and seeing the big picture, Capricorn really is the G.O.A.T.

So while he may be the most serious little sea goat that ever lived, I think there is an opportunity for welcoming in some irreverence and amusement this season. We all know by now that "all work and no play" can make us "dull," but the relentless demands of capitalism have convinced us that productivity must be constant and self-improvement should be an obsession. But sometimes we just need to be silly little billies! So this season we're going to buck the system a bit.

Just like billy goats balancing on a cliffside, we all need downtime and rest to offset the go-go-go attitude of our culture. You can't draw water from an empty well, even if you are part fish! An important part of any creative or productive practice is the part when you're NOT doing anything. We don't talk about it enough, but creativity cannot be constant. So instead of slipping into a shame spiral when we can't or don't feel like working, we can learn to appreciate that in order to fill up our cup, sometimes it has to start out empty.

One annoyingly spot-on piece of advice I got from my mother over the years was that I needed to try becoming a "human being" instead of a "human doing." Maybe it's my South Node in Capricorn, or maybe it's busyness as a trauma response, but in any case, she was right. If that resonates for you too, I hope this chapter will encourage you to create some space for rest and play, every single day!

TAKE A PERFECT POP-BACK-UP POWER NAP

One of the main secrets of my success is power napping. I take a nap almost every day. Anywhere between three-ish to six-ish in the afternoon, depending on my schedule for the day, is "lie-down time." A lot of people will say, "Oh, I can't nap! I always wake up feeling worse!" or "I can never fall asleep during the day!" And this is where my work as Nap Evangelist begins. I promise you that you *can* nap, you *will* feel better afterward, and it doesn't even actually matter if you fully fall asleep! But you have to follow the formula. It's adapted from Oprah's own personal napping technique, for crying out loud! So YOU take a nap! And YOU take a nap! And YOU take a nap!

STEP 1: Twenty minutes is all you need. You may want to carve out twenty to thirty to get set up and settled in, but you should close your eyes for only twenty minutes. Don't forget to set an alarm! Snooze at your own risk!

STEP 2: Make yourself comfortable . . . but not too comfortable! Wear soft, loose-fitting clothing if you can, but don't go full pajama. Depending on where you are in the world, maybe you can take an outer layer off or throw on a robe. Now, another crucial component is the blanket. Use a throw. On a couch? Use a throw. On your bed? Still use a throw. If you get all the way into bed and under the covers, it will be much harder to get up. I even have a dedicated nap blanket because I am extremely dedicated to napping.

STEP 3: It's lie-down time! Lie on your back and try to stay in that position. I find that this helps my body separate the idea

of napping from sleeping, since during the night I naturally sleep on my side. Start your alarm and close your eyes.

STEP 4: Wake up refreshed! Again, even if you didn't fall asleep (but I can almost guarantee that you will), a little meditation time never hurt anyone. In fact, just going through those motions and having a little quiet time to yourself is restful and beneficial, no matter what.

I find that these little twenty-minute breaks are exactly what I need to feel like I've still got some life left in me for the second half of the day, without feeling groggy. If you're still feeling a little restless, try setting a ten-minute sleep timer and listening to an audiobook or podcast.

SILLY LITTLE SNOW-GLOBE SPELL

Now that naptime is over, let's play around a bit before we shift into the more serious side of the season. Sometimes, even goats just wanna have fun! When we were kids, a lot of the time playing was our only job. Sometimes we wanted to be grown-ups so bad, and now we're like, "Ewww, why?" But the line between child you and adult you doesn't have to seem so stark. The idea of "putting childish things away" when you get older is one of those ideas that old, boring men came up with a trillion years ago that I would like us to divest from.

As times have gotten tougher since the start of the pandemic, one thing I turned to at the shop to keep it together was

prioritizing amusement. We were all asked to take on a lot of heavy, scary, life-or-death energy during those years, which wore down even the most responsible among us after a while. At HausWitch, once all of our safety bases were covered, we started saying "Yes!" to any idea that made our inner children giggle. Around the shop we started amassing a little coven of troll dolls to keep us company and even built them a little office by the cash register. Why? Just to bring some joy and irreverence into the Haus. Who was going to tell me I couldn't?

Amusement actually releases relaxation hormones. It's a state of nonjudgment, of delight in the present moment. The lost art of giving yourself permission to be goofy, or doing something just to do it. Allowing yourself to feel childish and irreverent is not only a great stress reliever but also a great way to practice anticapitalism. Taking a page from Black feminist poet Toi Derricotte, let's make "joy an act of resistance."[1]

In honor of this wintry month, let's create a reminder that taking ourselves too seriously can leave important qualities like curiosity, creativity, and fantasy out in the cold. We're going to bring the snowstorm inside by making a silly little snow globe, just because!

To get started, choose the object that you'll want as the center of attention. This could be a toy from your childhood or just something that feels light and amusing to you. Size is important here, so something in the two-to-three-inch range will work best. It's crucial that this little thing cheers you up when you see it! When I was writing this, I had recently found one of my oldest, most treasured toys, a plastic Glo Worm from the 1980s, dressed like a painter.

He was stuck in a box in my basement—a sad way for him to spend his retirement. I decided that transforming him into a life-inspiring delight was much more fitting. You may want to ask your toy (see Gemini season) whether it wants to be used in this way, just to make sure you're acting in alignment with its spirit. If you're not a borderline nostalgia-hoarder like me, you could instead find some seasonal figurines or plastic trees (as long as they make you smile!).

ACCESSORIES

- A clean jar with a lid. (A jar with eight to twelve ounces in capacity works well, but I've seen some real cuties made out of four-ounce baby food jars. Make sure the jar's sides are smooth, so that you can see all the snow swirling around!)
- Lint-free cloth for polishing

1   From the title of a poem, "Joy Is an Act of Resistance," by Toi Derricotte, an African American poet (born 1941).

- Sandpaper. (You'll want to rough up the lid, and possibly the bottom of your toy, a bit to help it attach securely. Really, any grit between 100 and 400 will do.)
- Figurines or toys. (Now this is the magickal part. Choose something that will remind you that, as Oscar Wilde said, "Life is far too important to be taken seriously.")
- Epoxy. (You'll need this water-resistant adhesive to permanently attach your toy or other figure(s) to the lid of the jar. Heavy-duty Gorilla Glue can work too; just make sure it's waterproof.)
- Distilled water. (This type of water does a good job of staying clear. Plain bottled water will work almost as well! The minerals and other materials in tap water can make it cloudy, so it's not such a good choice.)
- Glycerin. (This syrupy substance thickens the water just enough so the glitter falls more naturally, like snow. Vegetable glycerin is my go-to because it doesn't come from animal by-products.)
- Tinsel glitter. (Experiment with different glitters if you want, but I have found that white tinsel glitter works best because it looks most like snow.)

STEP 1: Clean your jar well, and wipe down with a lint-free cloth.
STEP 2: Scuff up the inside of the jar lid with the sandpaper.
STEP 3: Attach your toy to the inside of the lid with the epoxy. Let it dry overnight, or follow the instructions on the adhesive. While it's drying, spend a little time reflecting on the joyful feelings from childhood you can make space for in your adult life. Maybe watch an old episode of a cartoon or TV show you loved. Or jot down a few of your happiest, most mischievous memories in a journal. Charge

your toy (without moving it or touching it) with those intentions.

STEP 4: Next up, fill your jar with distilled water. Leave a little room for the water that will be displaced by the volume of the toy. (Whoa, some sixth-grade science stuff just burst out of my brain! Cool!)

STEP 5: Add a drop or two of glycerin to the water. If you have a big jar, you may want to use a little more. But be careful—adding too much can make the water thick and gloopy.

STEP 6: Add glitter to the jar. Start with a healthy pinch, and add more, depending on how snowy you want your snow globe to be. I use about half a teaspoon.

STEP 7: Now is the time! Screw on the lid with your little guy inside, flip the jar over, and let the bliss blizzard begin!

STEP 8: Give 'er a little shake any time you need a reminder to prioritize silliness!

SCHEDULING SORCERY

Okay, my little goats, it's time to bust out those pristine new planners and assign some magick to every day of the week. While some of these correspondences may be no-brainers, like SUNday and MOONday, every one of our seven days is ruled by a planet and therefore presents an opportunity to connect with otherworldly energies. I love this seamless, low-lift way to infuse some intention into every day.

SUNDAY: Ruled by . . . DUH, the sun, Sunday is the perfect time to let your light shine. Where do you want to glow up? Where do you need some illumination or inspiration? Today can be

a day to tap into your creative potential, or it can be a day to laze around like a baby sea goat in a sunbeam. It's about tapping into what you need to be your most authentic and aligned self. It might also be a good day to revisit the Gold Sun Meditation from Leo season! A weekly practice of filling up with your own unique neutral gold energy sounds like a great way to set yourself up for success in the week to come.

MONDAY: Moonday definitely gets a tough rap, whether it's "manic Monday" or "you've got a case of the Mondays." The back-to-reality vibes are strong. Ruled by the moon means emotions may be running high, so why not have yourself a good cry? I'm serious! Emotions need their own space, or they can take over in places you don't want them. Or, since Mondays are already so stressful, don't add more than you need to your plate. Instead, try some moon gazing! Tap into your intuition for answers, and make space for mystery! Just like the lunar phases, our weeks are cyclical too. Ask yourself, *How does my schedule for the week ahead flow? Am I steering the ship or just along for the ride?* Wear silver for an extra moon-boost.

TUESDAY: Now, today is the day to really get going. Ruled by Mars, it's a time to tap into some fire energy and make serious moves. Start something new! Stop procrastinating! Carpe diem! If there's something you dread doing every week, Tuesday is the time for it. Take out the trash! Clean out the car! Do the laundry! Start a war with procrastination, and claim victory over chores! Already a clean freak? Use Tuesday as a day for a fresh start. The key word here is "momentum," and if you can channel it today, you can keep it moving all week. Eat something orange or spicy to bring the fire to your belly.

WEDNESDAY: Hump day is a tricky one, since it's ruled by Mercury—that silly little imp always makes life more interesting. Expression and communication both get a boost today, so think a little about where your words could be more impeccable. If our thoughts can help shape our reality (and I believe they can), then certainly our words are just as powerful. How are you the messenger of your own story? Create an incantation that affirms a positive relationship between you and your self. On a more practical level, tackle your inbox and catch up on correspondence. It's also the right time to have that "we need to talk" talk. As my friend Janine says, "Hard conversations, easy life."

THURSDAY: By Jove! We made it to Jupiter day! Expand! Explore! Experiment! Go big! Go bold! Use too many exclamation points!!!! I think Thursday is my favorite day because, like the biggest planet in the solar system, it's about t a k i n g u p s p a c e. It's a great time to cast abundance spells. Start a prosperity piggy bank, and always add to it on Thursdays, even if it's just a penny! It's also a great day to be a little adventurous, so if you have errands to run that aren't close to home, save them for Thursdays. Go on a sidequest or try a new route home from work. Put a big red spot on your calendar to remind you.

FRIDAY: Oh, how my staff and I love Venus day. We all feel a little prettier, more sensual, and romantic. Things just feel softer and sparklier. Of course it doesn't hurt that we're headed into the weekend. (Not that the retail business observes weekends, but maybe your work does!) Buy yourself some flowers. Shop for some new clothes or makeup. Take a nice long bath. See your friends and show one another some mutual admiration. Tell someone you love them. Tell yourself! Stop and smell the roses. Make pleasure a priority!

SATURDAY: So, you're not going to want to hear this, but like Capricorn, Saturday is ruled by Saturn, and Saturn means business. Now, I definitely want you to build in some time for a little R&R today, especially if you work a Monday–Friday gig, but also make some time to check in with your boundaries. Did you give away any of your authority this week? Recommit to your routines. Structure creates a container for creativity. Saturdays are also great for clearing and banishing, so just like the phase of the dark moon, today is a great day to release. Clean out the fridge, shred that junk mail, do anything you need to clear a path to a successful new week ahead! Then channel Saturn and hula-hoop! Just kidding! Or am I?

Now that you have a rundown of each day's correspondences, you can create your own planetary planner! Make a photocopy, or print out one week of a weekly calendar. If you're more of a digital native than me, this can of course be done on a computer or through an app, I'm sure. Brainstorm ways you can work with the planets and maybe jot down a few key words at the top to help you along the way.

Now divvy up your responsibilities and commitments, based on which day best matches the vibe of each task. Don't worry about practicality for a sec. Just see if there's room in your life for some radical rescheduling!

MONEY MATTERS!

Since we're on the topic of responsibilities, I asked my friend the Money Witch to give her expert advice on budgeting—not just for yourself, but for the greater good! I've been seeking her advice for both my business and personal finances for years, and not only has she never steered me wrong, but she has helped me heal and transform my financial life. Plus she's amongst the coolest people you'll ever meet.

Take it away, Jessie Susannah!

BUDGETING FOR LIBERATION

by Jessie Susannah Karnatz, the Money Witch

This piece is inspired by a social media exchange with Uhuru Moor of the Uhuru Dreamhouse—a housing justice organization created by, maintained by, and serving Black and Indigenous trans people in Bulbancha, colonially known as New Orleans, Louisiana.

Capricorns are the leaders of finding meaning and satisfaction in tasks the rest of us may consider a real drag. Let's give the Capricorns what they want and take a moment to bring our intention obsession to . . . our finances! Capricorns care about sustainability and money is the fuel that gets your whole life where it needs to go.

Take a deep breath and get ready to shift your perspective. Instead of a bummer or a necessary evil, consider your budget to be an act of self-care and an act of community care.

Taking care of your budget prepares you to be a more potent contributor to liberation. Mutual aid, elder care, reparative giving, and resource redistribution all require us to manage our money with more clarity and maturity.

Budgets and other money work can take us straight to the shame shack—we feel ashamed of our lack of literacy, our failed past attempts at money management, all the ways we've failed to measure up to capitalist-colonial concepts of success. There is also grief present from our ancestors' experiences with money and resources and the trickle-down effect to our given family. So take a moment to wave hello to all those feelings—fear, anxiety, guilt, disappointment, rage, inadequacy—and accept that they live in your emotions and in your financial life. They are part of your history, but they don't have to shut you down.

Another block many sensitive and aware people encounter is avoiding personal financial management as an attempt to avoid exposure to or involvement in capitalism. It makes the most sense to want to distance yourself from this system and the impacts it has on the earth and on our lives (with disproportionate impact, depending on where in the intersectional matrix of power we're standing—credit to Kimberlé Crenshaw). Let me get my bedazzled bullhorn to tell you so loud: MISTREATING AND DISREGARDING YOUR PERSONAL FINANCES DOES ABSOLUTELY NOTHING TO DESTROY CAPITALISM. Okay, back to my inside voice. Ignoring your personal finances prevents you from occupying the edge of your sovereignty within capitalism. It has no positive impact at all on systemic inequality. Honestly, not having

systems and a plan for your finances means you sacrifice more money (via penalties and fees) and energy (via ongoing crisis management) on the altar of capitalism in the long run.

It's easy to let guilt and shame and confusion lead to overwhelm, which leads to inaction. But we're reclaiming our personal power in order to better participate in the power-with-not-power-over world we want to co-create. Whoever said "Don't be sorry, be better" was probably a Capricorn. What they mean is—it's perfectly human to get out of alignment with our purpose AND it's the human assignment to keep remembering our way back toward divine order and liberation. If you're a person of privileged experience, not having a grasp on your budget makes it much harder to contribute financially in a consistent and effective way. The Hebrew word "tzedakah" is one of my favorites to highlight the connection between finances and spirituality. Often translated as meaning "charity," it really means something more like distributing your money in a way that aligns with divine reality. Divine reality is that every living being deserves care, safety, agency, and the resources to make it happen.

Let me get that bullhorn out again: people of privilege, we have GOT to systematize our reparative giving! Reparations comes up like clockwork several times a year as a hot content topic and brings a flurry of urgent reposting with it. When these moments arise, infographics proliferate on our social media platforms. Many of us resonate and agree with the divine truth of economic repair for racialized economic injury. We hit the like button, we share it, we comment to affirm, and we feel the truth and resonance of the statement in our hearts. But there's a sharp decline between the number of people who like and share

and those that actually make the donation or a tangible plan to donate. We could call it performative (and YES, there's shadow work to dig into here, it's a both/and) but it's also just a struggle to get in integrity. Integrity means aligning your actions with your values and priorities. A huge reason for this gap between those who care about reparations and those who consistently show up to give well is that most people do not have their personal finances organized and systematized enough to be ready to follow through.

If we get in even deeper, connecting reparative giving and urgency is in itself perpetuating a form of violence. When we only give reparatively as an impulse or in reaction to a moment of social urgency, it puts marginalized people in the position of having to constantly evoke a reactivity of care from privileged people. This is a cycle that must be broken. It is degrading, exhausting, a waste of people's time and energy and precious life force, and surely not what people of marginalized experience need to spend their time on. The whole point is liberation and care! Racial economic disparity is an ongoing part of the systems we live in, not something that pops up as a surprise hot topic a few times a year. A predictable need deserves an organized response. More intentionality and less reactivity in your finances is going to bring you blessing, and is going to allow you to share that blessing with others who deserve it. Giving intuitively might feel more organic and "in flow," but it's not the most effective and respectful to the recipients. Mutual aid that is predictable and in the context of a committed relationship between the parties creates safety and community.

So let's get organized! If we're going to systematize our reparative giving, then we need systems, right? All financial plans begin with budgeting. Want to save, give, invest, or pay off debt? You have to know how much money you have after your monthly expenses to make it happen. A budget is just a documentation of what money came in and from where and what money went out and to where. Start with what I call a snapshot budget—going back to the last month (or three or six) and documenting where the money went. You are welcome to use a budgeting app if you like, but I love an old-fashioned spreadsheet. Download the .csv transaction files for your bank accounts and credit cards, and double-check you're only getting the transactions from the month you're documenting. Then assign each to a category and sort them out to get a clear picture of what you spent and on what.

As we mentioned earlier, money work can be very activating to the nervous system. Before you start, take a moment to set your space up, take a couple deep breaths. Tap in a couple of tools for nervous system support—a nervine tincture, a somatic exercise, a stone you find grounding—I love obsidian for this. Even though money can feel so spun out and dissociative within capitalism, money is archetypally linked with the earth element, so we have this ancestral invitation to get grounded and connect with earth before, during, and after our budgeting work. Remember that your financial tasks don't have to be ugly—get some nice file folders, highlighters, a pretty notebook. Buying and using new office supplies during Capricorn season is living the dream. Take a moment to bring intentionality to your money space—light a money candle, burn some herbs, pull out a tarot card you find inspiring (the Queen of Pentacles absolutely loves to help with budgets). Work with a friend for camaraderie, accountability, and co-regulating.

Don't assign judgment to your past financial decisions. Stand in forgiveness in order to move forward with intention. Most people live paycheck to paycheck, and there is no shame in that game. We just want to make sure that your hard-earned dollars are being used intentionally. How much is left in your budget after you pay your monthly bills and set aside a monthly portion toward your periodic expenses (such as car repairs, medical appointments, or taxes)? How much of that would you like to give to community members via mutual aid or reparative giving? Now that you have the numbers, what can you do to systematize that giving, so that it happens consistently and automatically? It's okay if what you have to give is five dollars a month. If our communities all show up consistently and we all pitch in our five dollars, we can do a lot to alleviate one another's suffering within this inhumane economic paradigm. And if you have more, that's beautiful and very welcome. We're not being perfectionists, we're challenging ourselves to be responsive when and how we're able. As Kenneth Jones and Tema Okun articulated, perfectionism is itself a characteristic of white supremacy culture. Perfectionism and "purity" are not liberatory because they are not humane. We're not going to get this perfect, but we are going to show up and participate, with intention!

The moral of the story (and Gxddess knows Capricorn loves a moral) is that doing the work of getting present with your finances makes you a more potent community member. Take a look at what habits, negative self-beliefs, and woundings are standing in your way of intentionality in your relationship with money. Just like any growth and healing work, it can get shadowy and difficult, but the results are always worth it. I see you wanting to be a potent contributor to liberation and

stepping up to do the hard work of being ready. Capricorn wants us to reach our full human excellence, and you are well on your way.

Okay, kids, I can barely contain my excitement because now we're headed out of this world to Aquarius season!

Aquarius
Season

Containing Multitudes

January 20—February 18

- **SYMBOL:** The Water Bearer
- **DEITY/PLANET:** Uranus
- **ELEMENT:** Air
- **TAROT SUIT:** Swords

- **BODY CONNECTION:** Circulatory system
- **CRYSTAL:** Labradorite

People don't always know what to make of Aquarius, and I get why. Is it an air sign? Is it a water sign? What's it all about? Humanity? Wisdom? Technology? The very fabric of space-time itself? Those are some pretty big and boundless concepts to fit in your jug! But not for the water bearers; they're right at home pouring out the secrets of the multiverse from their cosmic corner of the sky. I've heard it said that Aquarians are like aliens in human suits, and I must admit they can certainly seem otherworldly. They're visionaries, constantly creating their own new worlds just by refusing to conform to this one. In fact, Aquarius is so innovative that many believe that the Age of Aquarius will usher in a new paradigm for humanity in general! More on that in a bit . . .

If Capricorn is known for seeing the big picture, then Aquarius zooms out even farther and sees the *big-bang* picture.

With a POV that's always looking forward, Aquarius is ahead of its time, patiently waiting for the rest of us to catch up. Despite being the water bearer, Aquarius is an air sign, meaning the world of ideas, mental stimulation, and experimentation are all within its zone of excellence. But unlike Gemini, Aquarius is about doling out knowledge from the top down, rather than collecting messages from different dimensions. If Gemini is like an interesting conversation with a good friend, Aquarius is a fascinating lesson from your favorite teacher.

Mythologically, the water suggested in the name Aquarius is the wisdom of the gods being spilled out by this "cup bearer" to the stars. Not interested in gatekeeping the secrets of the universe, the water bearer's jug, like a watering can of new ideas, runneth over, and we all benefit. All of us on earth are like little seedlings thirsty for Aquarius's brand of innovation and invention. This constellation has long been a light guiding humanity toward what's next.

Among a million other questions, Aquarius season asks, both literally and metaphorically, What are you creating containers for in your life? Are you making space for the life you want, or is clutter clogging your clarity? Is there room for curiosity, creativity, movement, and flow? These life-affirming concepts are important, no matter who you are in daily life.

If you feel like your intentions are always falling to the wayside, maybe it's because there's no room for them to thrive. Sometimes things that feel impossible magickally manifest once a path is cleared. Trust me when I say that often the most magickal ingredient for creativity is an empty page or a clean desk. Or an hour carved out specifically devoted to letting your mind wander to the farthest reaches of the multiverse . . .

IMBOLC INVIGORATION SPELL

In the Northern Hemisphere, Aquarius season is deep in the heart of winter, which many of us spend cooped up in our homes for months on end. Even we hard-core Haus cats feel a little stiff-bodied and stir-crazy by late January. Our senses are calibrated to take in the natural world, but when we're inside for too long, they can dull. So, with this ritual, we're bundling up and going outside, to raise our heart rate and recalibrate! The part of the body associated with Aquarius is the circulatory system, so let's get that blood pumping again and reconnect with nature while we're at it.

The perfect time to perform this spell is on or around Imbolc, a pagan holiday that falls on February 1, halfway between the Winter Solstice and the Spring Equinox. Historically this was a time to take stock of what resources were left to get through winter and what to leave behind heading into spring. So it's the perfect time to check in with your body and let the fresh air breathe some new life into your veins.

Everyone has different levels of mobility, so please tailor this ritual to your own needs and abilities. If walking isn't accessible to you, sitting somewhere outside and moving your body in any way will be perfect!

1. Decide how long you can be outside, and then divide the number of minutes by six. For example, I can commit to being even slightly cold only for thirty minutes. So this allows me six five-minute intervals.

2. Before going outdoors, find a little food to bring with you. Maybe just a raisin, or a mint.

3. Find a path or a park or even a backyard that situates you in nature. Try to visually block out anything human-made.

4. Set a timer based on the length of one interval.

5. Set an intention, or think of a question you want answered.

6. Get moving! Begin walking (or shimmying in place), and start your timer. For your first interval, take in everything you can with your sense of sight. If you're on a familiar path, you might notice something you've never seen before. If you're staying in one place, what stands out to you when you look around?

7. After this interval has passed, reset the timer, and now focus on your sense of smell. Does the air smell like snow? Or smoke from a fireplace? Maybe you're actually somewhere warm (if so, I'm very jealous), and the air smells like flowers. Just notice.

8. For the third interval, pay attention to what you hear. Your own footsteps crunching on the leaves or snow? Animal friends chatting with each other? Just listen.

9. Next up is touch. How does the air feel on your skin? Is there a tree you can hug or give a gentle pat?

10. For the fifth interval, focus on taste. Mindfully eat the food you brought. Or maybe even taste a little (clean) ice or snow.

11. Finally, for the last interval, reconnect with your intention or question, and do a bit of nature scrying. Look for signs, listen for answers! Do you feel clearer? What does your shadow have to say?

12. Thank nature for all it does and all it is.

13. Go back home, and warm up with some hot tea or soup! Thank your body for all it does and all it is!

JUG LIFE

While the water bearer may have a vast vessel holding the secrets of the universe, we witches have the next best thing . . . JARS! If you've read the rest of this book, then you already know that, to a witch, an empty jar holds a world of possibilities. We've filled them with scrubs and teas, created spell bottles and snow globes. But for this next set of spells, we're going to embrace empty space and make sure the jar is the star.

So, we're already familiar with the basic technology of the jar spell from Libra season: put a bunch of stuff in a bottle or jar to create a desired effect. We are going to expand on that idea yet also leave room for the magick of the universe to flow in! For each of these spells, choose a jar big enough to hold the desired ingredients while leaving the jar half empty. All of the practical ingredients in the world won't mean much without a little magickal mystery!

There are many different spells you can cast with vessels, and most of them are based on magickal correspondences of the ingredients. The most

powerful way to approach them is to use the ingredients that make the most sense to you. If the correspondence of cinnamon with abundance resonates with you, use that in your manifesting spells. If basil feels more luxurious and symbolic of success to you, use that. Heck, use 'em both! I'll give you some foundational ingredients of basic jar spells, but the specifics are up to you and should be as nuanced as possible.

A lot of jar spells I've seen on the internet might involve messing with the energy or free will of another person, and I personally would caution against that. If you are trying to attract a certain person, or banish someone from your life, I would encourage you to reframe your spell to make yourself the only direct recipient of the energy you're conjuring. In the case of attracting, I would make the spell about feeling more attract-ive. In the case of banishing, I would think of it as a personal clearing of any relationship that's no longer serving your best interests, rather than an energetic confrontation with another person.

I believe that practicing ethical witchcraft means staying in your own energetic lane and respecting everyone's energetic autonomy. Furthermore, when we try to force or impose our will on someone else, we're giving our energy away to them, and who knows what they'll do with it! It's just not a good idea. See also Nancy from *The Craft*.

JAR SPELL STARTERS

- **HONEY:** Sweetener spell jars are super popular. I've heard of them used for everything from winning court cases to attracting love or money. We're not here to force, we're here to draw things to us. Much like the old saying "You catch more flies with honey than vinegar." Which brings me to . . .

- **VINEGAR:** For the opposite side of the coin, many witches use vinegar to sour something that they want to decrease. Vinegar, lemon juice, and (it has to be said) urine are all good for purposes of curse breaking or banishing.

- **OIL:** I like the idea of using oil of any kind to represent ease. Add a little to your spell to grease those cosmic wheels.

- **MOONWATER:** Use moonwater charged under a specific sign or phase matching your intention.

- **WRITTEN INTENTIONS OR SIGILS:** Putting a piece of paper with a magickal mission statement or sigil at the bottom of your jar can help clarify your magickal intent.

- **HERBS:** If you're looking to grow or preserve something, herbs are the way to go. If you're on the growing side, use fresh herbs; if you're trying to maintain something, use dried. If there's anything witches love more than jars, it's herbs, so check out Taurus season if you need a refresher on some common traditional correspondences.

- **CRYSTALS:** Okay, okay, as far as magickal ingredients go, witches also really love crystals a lot. These sparkling beauties are like magick solidified. The easiest way to match a crystal to your magickal intent is by color. Go back to Leo season to see the traditional correspondences, or better yet, create your own!

- **OBJECTS:** Material items that represent your intention are the most direct and literal way to let the universe know what you're looking for. Trying to quit smoking? Drop a cigarette in the jar and pour vinegar on it. Trying to attract abundance? Some coins and honey might help money stick to you like glue!

- **AIR:** Okay, here's where I make the case for leaving space in your spell jar to symbolize the fact that we are co-creators with the universe. If your money space is always filled

with worry, is there room for abundance to flow in? If you're still energetically attached to an old flame, how will you create sparks with a new one? I hope I've convinced you in the past eleven chapters that even witches, with all our esoteric knowledge and secret skills, do not control, well, really anything besides our own energy and intentions. All we can do is try to nudge the energy where we want it to go with willpower and accommodation, and the rest is up to spirit. Let that liberate you to let go and invite flow.

ACCESSORIES

- 1 jar of any size (An old mason jar or jelly jar is perfect.)
- Squares of material matched to your intention, such as fabric, cheesecloth, or even a coffee filter—just something porous to put on top of the jar before sealing it with the lid
- Rubber bands to hold the fabric on the jar
- Candle or ribbon for sealing
- Empty space!

"A FUTURE SO BRIGHT" JAR SPELL FOR ROAD OPENING

Start with some oil charged under an Aries or Sagittarius moon to grease your witch wheels a bit. Use yellow fabric to connect to your solar plexus, your willpower center. Use herbs and other ingredients that relate to your goals or aspirations. Don't forget to leave room for happy accidents!

"ARMS OUTSTRETCHED" JAR SPELL FOR RECEIVING ABUNDANCE

Let the universe know you're ready to receive. Find a lucky penny on the street to acknowledge the little gifts that are all around you. Add a magnet to draw in more, and use green fabric to remind your heart to stay open! Top it off with honey to make your intention stick.

"POUR ONE OUT" JAR FOR RELEASING RESISTANCE

For this souring spell, use the vinegar to alchemize something you're ready to release. Use black or red fabric to ground yourself in your power. After the full moon, pour your spell down the toilet or the drain, and feel the sweet relief of release!

TECH SPELLS

Aquarius is another sign, like Scorpio and Pisces, with two different ruling planets. Traditionally, Aquarius was ruled by Saturn, which gives Aquarians naturally good boundaries and a healthy level of discipline for the things they're dedicated to. When Uranus (pronounced with a short "a," btw) was discovered by astronomers in 1781, it felt like a better fit for nonconforming Aquarius. I mean, for one thing, the planet itself is completely *tilted* on its axis. A lot of the planets are a little wonky in this regard, but Uranus takes it to an extreme by rotating on its side at a ninety-seven-degree angle, and also backward. What a rebel!

Because Uranus was the first planet discovered in "modern" times, it is associated with science, discovery, and new technology, such as the internet. This lines up perfectly with Aquarius's big-picture view of humanity and what connects us. There's no doubt that the internet can be used for good, bad, and ugly, but did you know it can also be used for witchcraft?

Aside from being a vast resource for information about spells and magick, the internet and our devices connected to it can be part of the spell work itself. If you've ever arranged emojis intentionally in a text message, you're basically already doing it! I don't really know that much about AI, but it definitely seems like some kind of magick (that I'm a little scared of . . .). Here are a few more ideas for channeling the vibes of this tech-savvy time of year.

INTENTIONAL PASSWORDS:
This is one I swear by. We type in our passwords a million times a day, so why not make them manifesting spells? Be specific! Instead of just "money777,"

make it an exact amount. I have doubled my income twice since making a password to a website I use a lot: "Doublemyincome" followed by the number I'm trying for. No joke. You can use different ones for different types of accounts. Maybe your online dating account is a tiny love letter to your future partner? Maybe your social media password has the number of followers you want? What better way to tell the universe what you want, over and over again, every single day!

LOCK SCREEN SPELLS: Along the same lines, your lock screen/ desktop background gets a lot of attention too. Which gives us a great opportunity to infuse it with some INtention! Images are like portals, and just seeing them can reinforce subtle energetic connections in your brain and influence shifts in consciousness. Make your lock screen a tarot card you've pulled recently or one that holds an archetype you're trying to embody. Maybe a cool photo of a crystal you're working with or a collage of images that illustrate the mechanics of your spell. Switch these out when you feel like they're not activating your brain every time you see them.

EMAIL CLEANSE AND UNSUBSCRIBE: Let's be honest, this will probably clear more energy in your life than any amount of burning herbs ever could. Clear out that inbox, unsubscribe from spam, and delete the junk. Do it during a waning moon and say *"I unsubscribe from this vibe"* as often as you want—just to make it a little more fun!

GENIUS PARTY

Did you know that in ancient Rome everyone had a genius? Unlike today's concept, genius wasn't something you are, but rather something you have. Sort of like a guardian angel or a muse, but not quite. There were many types of geniuses too—geniuses for music and art, for cooking, athletics, making crops grow, and hosting successful festivals and celebrations. Aquarians are often thought of as the (mad) geniuses of the zodiac, so it's the perfect time to meet yours. Who are they? How do they communicate with you? How can they help you thrive?

A few years ago I had a reading where I was told that my genius liked to whisper in my ear using a datura flower (also known as angel's trumpet), which looks something like an old gramophone record player. Now I keep a bottle of datura essence on my desk and take a drop when I need to remember to quiet my brain and listen for my genius. Other times, I have to make more of an effort. One of the ways I like to engage is by hosting a Genius Party! This is usually just intentionally engaging with something I'm interested in or drawn to, like watching a documentary or binging a podcast series. But my favorite way is going down a "wisdom wormhole."

WISDOM WORMHOLE

Try this when the moon is in one of the more curious signs: Aquarius, Gemini, or Sagittarius.

For this ritual you're going to do a deep dive into one subject that interests you, for ONE HOUR. The time limit helps create a container for curiosity, so you won't fall into a scroll-hole or spend half the day on Wikipedia. Use a timer to help set this boundary.

Start by picking a topic. You may want to have a running list of "I wonder why" thoughts going throughout the month. Or maybe you already have things you've always wanted to know more about. This can be anything from how crystals are formed, to your own birth chart, to the Great Cleveland Balloon Disaster of 1986. The options are truly infinite!

If you're having trouble getting started, the app Stumble Upon connects you to the "hidden gems of the internet" that will leave you wanting to learn

more. Wikipedia is also a great resource (just remember that randos can edit Wikipedia pages with very little oversight). If there's a juicy nonfiction book collecting dust on your shelf, this is the perfect time to crack it.

Start by dropping in and greeting your genius.

Start your timer.

Go!

THE AGE OF AQUARIUS, THE "NEW AGE"

One of many wisdom wormholes I've gone down to write this book was researching the dawning of a "new age," the Age of Aquarius. Astrologers believe this will be a time when the Aquarian concepts of technological innovation, consciousness-raising, and humanitarianism will usher in a new paradigm for humankind. My interest was first piqued in a workshop about Jungian perspectives on this new age, and how the humanity-uniting themes of Aquarius are already making their way into the cultural zeitgeist. It was fascinating, and I'll do my best to give you the CliffsNotes version.

Let's hop in a time machine and talk about astrological ages. Basically, astronomers believe that the earth goes through astrological epochs called the Procession of the Equinoxes every 2,160-ish years. (For ease's sake, let's round down to about 2,000—these things are not an exact science anyway, as we'll see.) This is how long it takes for the Spring Equinox to move *backward* through the zodiac from one constellation to the next. Do not ask me to explain what that means because I definitely do not fully understand it, but that's what it is, in the simplest terms. These epochs coincided with collective shifts in human consciousness over the past eight millennia. All right, back to the time machine, we're headed waaaaaaay back, about eight thousand years!!!!

(Pretend we're in a real wormhole, going at the speed of light!! Cosmic colors! Swirly lights! Threads of the universe!)

AGE OF GEMINI, 6000–4000 BCE

Okay! Here we are, at the beginning of recorded history.[1] It's only right that at the very end of the Gemini era, around 4000 BCE, written language was invented. But throughout those two thousand years, humans were evolving to use language in new and inventive ways. Which is like, so Gemini, don't you think?

AGE OF TAURUS, 4000–2000 BCE

Now we're going to breeze through the epoch of Taurus, dominated by golden calf worship and cosmic bull imagery. During this period humans really settled into the agricultural revolution and started forming civilizations in the "fertile crescent." Living off the land in a new way and domesticating animals marked a pretty huge shift for the human race, one that lines up perfectly with the vibes of Taurus.

AGE OF ARIES, 2000 BCE–1 CE

Next up is Aries, a time of strong patriarchal leadership and male-dominated monotheism, like Judaism. The shofar, a musical instrument used in important Jewish ceremonies, is made from a ram's horn.

The widespread wars of conquest in Greece and Rome around this time also perfectly exemplify that hot-tempered Aries energy.

AGE OF PISCES, 1 CE–PRESENT DAY?

And now let's come back to the Age of Pisces, which we're currently in. (Maybe?) This age is symbolized by the fish, also one of the symbols of Christianity (ever heard of it?). This religious paradigm, which has dominated the last 2000-ish years, carries

---

1   Anything before that is hard to know much about. Because writing wasn't yet invented, there are no written records, but it's safe to say that the Age of Cancer coincides with a time where moon worship and familial bonds were more important than ever for survival. See also matriarchy.

themes of martyrdom, suffering, and stark binaries, like good versus evil. It is an era in which those values have colonized the globe. It's not all bad, though. Humanity is more connected than ever, and an explosion of cultural artifacts, artistic expression, and abstract thinking has made this epoch, shall we say, moody and complex?

So when does the Age of Aquarius start? Some people think it's already here! Because no one really, totally agrees when specifically to start the astro-calendar, and because the 2,160-ish year thing is sort of a guesstimate. Some folks think this tech-savvy age actually started with the discovery of our friend Uranus in 1781! Those folks see the past few hundred years of scientific revolution and technological "advances" as a clear sign that the Aquarian Age has already begun. But most place the beginning much closer to now—some with the invention of the internet, some with the seven-planet stellium in Aquarius in 2021.[2] Others believe it won't happen for another 100 to 150 years. Either way, it's safe to say that we're in a transition period, and those can last awhile . . .

Which reminds me of a quote by the Marxist philosopher (and Aquarius!) Antonio Gramsci: "The old world is dying and the new world struggles to be born; now is the time of monsters." And while I hesitate to refer to *all* of us as monsters, I think it's safe to say that there are some monstrous things happening all around us. This is because unlike, say, the Procession of the Equinoxes (which sounds so cool, I think I just like saying it now), human progress is not linear. History repeats itself all

the time, and we're currently dealing with a severe backlash against progressive ideals. The rise of contemporary fascism, the need to dominate and control people's bodies, and the ever-growing wealth disparity between rich and poor are just a few ways that we seem to be regressing.

For me, any movement that isn't focused on taking care of people is backward. Anything in opposition to the goal of liberation for all life on earth and bringing humanity together to tackle global issues causes harm. Capitalism would have us believe that we've made incredible progress over the past hundred years or so just because developments in technology, medicine, and consumerism have raised the quality of life for *some*. But that has come

2   In late January 2021, the sun, moon, Mercury, Venus, Jupiter, and Saturn were all lined up in Aquarius. This came soon after the Grand Conjunction of Jupiter and Saturn on the Winter Solstice in 2020. Many believed this series of astro-events marked the gateway to the Age of Aquarius. Including me!

at the expense of many other nations' resources being stolen and exploited, leaving their people impoverished. Is it really progress if people all over the world still go hungry every day? Why isn't the project of housing people and making sure they have fresh water considered more important than developing new weapons of war? Why are we still burning fossil fuels when science and technology have told us that they are destroying the planet? We did away with royalty and aristocracy, but now billionaires hoard wealth like the kings and queens of old, while sowing division among the working classes, so that solidarity of the many will never be strong enough to take back power from a greedy, despicable few. Don't you think we should really know better by now?

So let's stop those regressive values dead in their tracks with a nice little freezer spell in honor of this cold, wintry season. If we're preparing for a New Age, we can't be bogged down rehashing the old one! But don't worry, this spell is nowhere near as complicated as describing the Age of Aquarius. The hardest part will be deciding which backward-leaning issue to deep-freeze. For extra Aquarian credit, find an actual anti-progressive bill or piece of legislation local to you, and cast your spell on it.

One reason we're going to focus on systems and institutions is that I personally believe that binding spells on actual people is a bad idea. As we noted concerning jar spells, messing with the life and free will of another person feels wrong. We can't force change on or bind other people. We can and should focus only on ourselves and the matrices of power that mediate our lives. However, institutions like, say, the Supreme Court are fair game as far as I'm concerned.

"NO GOING BACK"
FREEZER SPELL

ACCESSORIES

- Black candle
- Paper
- Pen
- Rubber band or string
- A freezable container (This could be a jar, a Tupperware container, or even a plastic freezer bag. Avoid glass, as it can shatter in the freezer.)
- Freezer

1. On a night when the moon is waning, gather all of your accessories in front of you, and light the candle.

2. Write on your paper the anti-Aquarian law, regressive institution, legislation, or general idea that you want to freeze.

3. Place both hands, palms down, over the paper and say the incantation on the opposite page.

4. Carefully cover the words written on the paper with a few drops of wax from your candle to seal the incantation.

5. Now roll the paper into a scroll, and tie your string or secure your rubber band around it.

6. Place the paper in the container, and fill with water.

7. Place the spell in the freezer, toward the back so it won't get in the way. Forget about it if you want, or thaw and refresh the spell during the next waning moon.

Okay, I hope your jug feels full because it's time for some serious dreaming and scheming in watery Pisces season!

With the power of this charm,
I bind you from causing harm,
Freezing you in place.
I protect the human race
From a backward crawl,
Brightening the future for us all.

Pisces Season

A Whole Mood

February 19—March 20

- **SYMBOL:** The Fish
- **DEITY/PLANET:** Neptune
- **ELEMENT:** Water

- **TAROT SUIT:** Cups
- **BODY CONNECTION:** Feet
- **CRYSTAL:** Aquamarine

Welcome to the mystical realm of Pisces! Life is but a dream in this water-colored season! Pisces is the sign of imagination, intuition, and boundless creativity. But the word that always comes to mind for me, a Pisces moon, is *swirly*. Sort of like the brushstrokes in a van Gogh painting. What wiggly, wavy Pisces lacks in structure, it makes up for in interdimensional knowing and a mastery of fluidity.

It's the wee hours of the morning as I write this. I'm having to squeeze writing into odd times of day as my deadline for this book approaches. But who laughs in the face of deadlines, or limits in general? Pisces. Pisceans are the artists of the zodiac, and sometimes art takes time! In fact the day I started this chapter, I didn't get very far before I got completely sidetracked and spent hours watching dogs-reuniting-with-their-owners videos on TikTok and bawling my eyes out. Then I took a CBD bath and watched *Barbie*. Even though I didn't get any work done, I still felt immersed in Pisces season vibes.

Or maybe "submerged" is a better word for it. Pisces is a water sign, but unlike Cancer's day at the beach, or Scorpio's deep dive into dark waters, this season is all about the current itself, the way water moves and flows. The deep, amorphous force that makes seaweed seem to dance, while jellyfish jiggle and fish fly through the abyss.

Who better to navigate the surreal waters of Pisces season than fish? Mythologically, the symbol of the two fish was thought to represent Cupid and Venus, who dove into the water to save themselves from the monster Typhon. (That's the same Typhon that made Capricorn grow a fish tail! Man, that guy was a real menace.) Today we think of these fish as representing the dueling energies of above and below, conscious and unconscious, heaven and earth, beginnings and endings. Pisces is ruled by Neptune, a planet with no well-defined solid surface, made instead of water that is neither liquid or frozen; it exists in some mysterious third state.

Similarly, Pisces is the sign that doesn't so much blur binaries as transcend them. There is a whole world, an entire reality, between above and below. An entire subconscious realm between awake and asleep, and our entire human existence between heaven and earth. Pisces is a translator between these extremes, showing us these liminal spaces through the language of art, music, poetry, and dreams. Its truest gift is that of attunement, the ability to tap into feelings, energies, and everything in between.

So this month we're tuning in to all things Pisces. We're going to dive into the flowing magick of water spells, make some art to hone our intuition, decode our dreams, swim with the fishes, and finish out the year's cycle with a bang. Which, knowing the emotional nature of Pisces, may sound more like a whimper.

H2-WHOA! WATER SPELLS

One of my earliest memories comes from when I was about three years old. I was completely obsessed with the cartoon *Rainbow Brite*. (Did I let myself get distracted and watch a whole episode on YouTube just now? I think we all know the answer to that question.) Rainbow herself had an amazing rainbow belt, a horse that could run on rainbows, and a bunch of friends called the Color Kids. They all worked together to bring color to the world. Her sidekick, a sprite named Twink, had a pouch of Star Sprinkles, which they threw around to make rainbows wherever they went.

So back to a very earth-toned Indianapolis circa 1980-something, and I'm standing on my bed, throwing my own "star sprinkles" around. Much to my mother's dismay, they were made of tap water in a Ziploc bag, and I was completely soaking my bedroom. After asking what the hell I was doing, she came back with a bag of Fruity Pebbles. Even though they looked and felt much more like Rainbow Brite's colorful Star Sprinkles, the magick was gone by then, and I was uninterested. I think it's because using my imagination was more satisfying than being closer to reality. Or maybe because water felt magickal in a way that cereal just didn't.[1]

One of my all-time favorite quotes comes from martial arts master Bruce Lee, who said, "You must be shapeless, formless, like water. When you pour water in a cup, it becomes the cup.

---

1   Looking back, that would've caused a much bigger mess, crunching into crumbs in my bed and carpet, right?

When you pour water in a bottle, it becomes the bottle. When you pour water in a teapot, it becomes the teapot. Water can drip and it can crash. Become like water, my friend."

As a martial artist, Lee was deeply connected to his body. And the human body is about 60 percent water! When we can tune in to its deep, primeval wisdom, we can tap into some of the magick that lives inside us. Water comes in many forms to work with in spells, so I'm gonna give you some ideas for every one I can think of! Maybe you can imagine even more.

RAINWATER: You know that magickal intersection of rainy day and day off from work that has you curled up under a blanket with a mug

of something hot and a good book? Well, why not catch some rainwater in a bowl, add some lavender essential oil, and make a soothing rainy-day room spray for whenever you need to give yourself permission to rest and relax?

SNOW: Now, depending on where you are in the world, you may not have access to snow. Which sounds like both a blessing and a curse to this Midwesterner turned New Englander. Lately I've been doing a little snow-day ritual when blizzards roll through. I spend the day cooking something elaborate and comforting. But first I charge some of the ingredients out in the snow! The German goddess of snow is named Holda, and so I like to think she's blessing the ingredients before I use them. Cooking is a form of alchemy, after all.

Another snow spell would be to write out something you're looking to banish from your life in fresh white snow, and then sprinkle rock salt on it until the words dissolve away . . .

SEAWATER: Water from the sea isn't just salty, it's imbued with the powerful properties of a thousand myths and legends. Charge something organic, like a leaf, with intention, and then release it into the sea as a way of letting your intention be known to the universe. Or you could write it in the sand and let the tide take it from there.

SALTED WATER: Even if you don't live near the ocean, you can create your own seawater just by adding salt to water! Also, a salt circle is one of my favorite ways to create an energetic boundary, and if there's one thing Pisces could always use some help with, it's boundaries. Pisces's shadow energy can lead to self-abandonment and blurry transpersonal dynamics. Add some salt to a bath (or use a salt scrub in the shower), and then save a little bit of the water to sprinkle around your space to extend the protective vibes.

STORMWATER: Unlike relaxing rainwater, stormwater holds the properties of thunderbolts and lightning *(very, very frightening!)* as well. In a storm, the power of nature is on full display, and all of the elements are involved. The air and water of the clouds crashing together, the fire of the lightning, and the earth receiving it all below are all extremely activated during storms. I always think storm energy brings a sense of awe and wonder and can add a major boost of intensity to any of your spells. Carefully leave a bowl out to collect this supercharged water, and use it to amplify any spell.

TAP WATER: Good old tap water. Where would we be without you? I would put easy access to safe, clean, drinkable water at the top of the list of modern miracles and privileges. So if you are one of the fortunate folks around the globe to have it, make sure you give a little gratitude to our humble faucets. Then, use your tap water for something a little special, like a simmer pot!

To bring in sweetener spell vibes, charge up a few sugar cubes and then dissolve them in boiling tap water. Add some dried herbs like lavender, hibiscus, basil, or mint for extra intention (and taste!). After the mixture cools, strain through a cheesecloth, and use your magickal new simple syrup for manifesting spells and cocktails!

DEW: In my first-ever book of Wiccan spells there was a Beltane (May 1) spell that involved waking up at dawn and putting morning dew on your face to increase beauty. I would say, use it this way to *feel* more beautiful, because it's more likely that self-esteem will project outward than it is that the dew will somehow change your face. Whether you use it for beauty or something else, dew is basically faerie water, so make sure you thank the faeries for the little treat! You *do not* want to upset them!

TEARS: Tears are a powerful spell for release and movement, and our bodies (not to mention our spirits) need that from time to time. Crying activates the parasympathetic nervous system and releases endorphins and oxytocin. It also helps the body let go of stress hormones. So have yourself a nice Intentional Tantrum! Let it all out! Move that stuck emotional energy! There is literally no better time than Pisces season—take it from a Pisces Moon. I literally LOVE to cry. If you need a little help getting started, may I suggest videos of dogs being reunited with their owners?

PASTA WATER: And finally, pasta water. You may already know the magick trick of using a cup of the water you boiled your pasta in to help thicken your sauce and stick to the noodles, but did you know you can use it in a bunch of other ways as well? Reuse pasta water as a base for soups and stocks, in pizza dough, or for steaming vegetables. Also, watering your plants with pasta water gives your leafy little friends essential nutrients because it acts as a natural fertilizer! You can store pasta water in the fridge for up to three days or freeze it in ice cube trays! Imagine the pasta-bilities!

WOO-WOO WATERCOLORING

I mentioned that Pisceans are the artists of the zodiac, so what could be more aligned with the season than watercoloring! Painting is a relaxing activity that can put your brain in an alpha state, a light, relaxing trance that fosters creativity. Watercolors are a super accessible medium, and little to no skill is needed to enjoy it.

For this ritual we're going to take the idea of watercoloring deeper into the depths of Pisces season by creating a tool for tuning in to your intuition! Intuition is a kind of knowing, but it doesn't come from the conscious mind. Intuition is a kind of feeling, but it isn't an emotion. It's somewhere in between. Sort of like a thought you have to feel. Make sense? Intuition can guide you through all sorts of tough decisions, hard choices, or anything you can't quite find mental clarity on. Have you ever heard the saying "Gut feelings are guardian angels"?

Unfortunately we're not often taught to recognize these guardian angels, but as witches we know how important tapping into the sixth sense can be! Honing your intuition requires a certain amount of self-trust, so let's start intentionally building that with a mystical memory game.

ACCESSORIES

- Moonwater
- Watercolor paints
- Paintbrushes
- Watercolor paper, at least 8.5 × 11 inches in size
- Scissors or paper cutter
- Pencil or ballpoint pen

1. Choose six simple symbols, such as a circle, a square, a triangle, a figure eight, a couple of wavy lines, and a lightning bolt. You can certainly be more elaborate if you're better at drawing than I am!

2. Next, use moonwater to activate the paints, and go to town painting one whole side of a sheet of watercolor paper. For this ritual, the more abstract the better, but paint whatever you feel called to. If it takes a few tries to make something you really love, that's okay! Draw inspiration from dreams, your favorite colors, and so on.

3. Pay attention to the way the water moves, how it changes the consistency of the paints, how the colors swirl and blur on their own. Then let the painting dry.

4. After it dries, cut your painting into twelve equal-size rectangles or squares to create a set of cards.

5. Now lightly draw one of your symbols on two of your cards. It's important that the symbol does not show through to the other side of the paper, so use a pencil or ballpoint pen, not a marker. Or use the watercolors to paint them!

6. Repeat with the rest of the cards until you have two of each symbol, and all twelve cards are complete.

7. Now give your "deck" a quick shuffle, and turn all the cards symbol-side down in three rows of four.

8. Take a minute to drop in and connect with your intuition. Haven't met her yet? Well, now is the time. As you did with your genius, simply invite her in.

9. Float your hands, palm sides down, over the cards, and see if you can incorporate their energy into your own auric field. Imagine an orb of glowing, watercolor light

enveloping you and your cards.

10. Flip your first card over. Now concentrate on finding its match. Close your eyes. Feel into finding the matching card. Know that your sixth sense 100 percent knows which card it is—you just need to tap into it.

11. Flip a second card. If it's not the right one, don't judge yourself too harshly! Developing your intuition takes time and practice. Luckily, you're already working on it. Keep trying until you've flipped all twelve cards.

12. Practicing regularly will help you build a connection with your intuition and feel more confident trusting it when it counts!

SURREALITY BITES

Pisces rules the realm of dreams. What could be more Piscean than surreal messages from your unconscious that you can decode only with feelings? So whether you're a regular dreamer or not, there are a few things you can do to help connect your conscious and unconscious minds to unlock a whole new understanding of your psyche.

My own connection to dreams is somewhat liminal. I really struggle to remember anything from my dreams most of the time. I even work a lot of the magick I'm going to suggest to you here, and yet I still have trouble connecting to my dreams on a conscious level. However, the few and far-between dreams that I do remember have provided rich material to dive deeper into. So, no judgment if you also struggle with dream

magick. The thing I can say for sure is that even if you can't remember every detail, or if what you do recall seems too wild to hold any useful meaning, it's still worth setting some dream-related intentions. Especially during Pisces season.

Though my own dreamwork has been somewhat tenuous, dreams have still played a major role in my life and healing: my father came to me in a dream and encouraged me to open my shop. I saw a sort of montage flash before my eyes—images I couldn't totally understand—but I remember seeing exposed brick walls like the ones my shop has, and aura photos, and just general vibes of peace, love, and witchcraft. *It felt good.* Over it all was his voice saying, "If you want to open a store, it's time to open a store." I listened! The store opened a few months later and the rest is herstory.

For the past few years I've been having a recurring dream during

which I'm always late to the airport (of course, these would be the dreams I consistently remember). The circumstances are always different, but the theme is the same: the flight is in less than an hour, and I am still packing, or stuck in traffic, or other completely absurd things are happening as I frantically check the time and freak out over how I got so off track! In waking life, travel does feel pretty stressful to me, so I plan very meticulously. I am definitely a "get to the airport two hours ahead" kind of dad. I pack carefully, schedule a ride way ahead of time, and check the traffic on the route obsessively. So why do I have so many dreams where this all goes to hell? Well, I started tracking *when* I'm having these dreams, and that context provided more insight than just looking up the meaning of unpacked suitcases online. I noticed I was having those dreams during particularly stressful times, when I was feeling like things were a bit out of my control. Which meant that I could use the occurrence of these dreams as a way of signaling that I needed to do some stress management in my waking life.

Over my years of studying Carl Jung and his methods of psychoanalysis, and through working with my own analysts, I've learned that even if you don't put too much stock into what your dreams are trying to tell you, they are definitely trying to communicate *something*. Something I learned in a lecture that I find absolutely fascinating is the phenomenon of a "herald dream," one that usually comes when someone is about to start a new cycle in analysis; for newcomers to therapy, it usually occurs leading up to the first appointment with a therapist (for those already undergoing analysis, it can point toward a new direction needed in your sessions). It is rich in symbolism, a messenger that foreshadows what will come up in therapy.

I was so intrigued by this idea that I really tried to poke holes in it to make sure it was true. I asked the lecturer: "Okay, but I rarely have dreams, and it's even rarer that I remember them."

And the teacher replied: "You would still have a herald dream before entering analysis."

"Okay, but what if I already consciously knew what I wanted to be working on in therapy?"

"You would still have a herald dream."

"Okay, but I've been in therapy on and off for years, and dream analysis has never really played a role."

"You will still have a herald dream when you need to have one."

And of course, she was right. As I mentioned, I've been in therapy on and off for a long time, but now that I know to look out for them, I can see that I have had herald dreams before going back into therapy and also following a lull, when I feel like I'm not getting much out of my sessions. Next thing you know, I have a very long and vivid dream with details I can actually remember, and I know that there's some specific unconscious material that my conscious mind needs to address.

So, whether you're an easy dreamer or dreams always seem to be just out of reach, we have intentions to set and dreams to catch. First, we'll make sure our sleep space is set up to encourage dreaming with meaning, and then we'll create our own personal primers for decoding them!

NIGHTSTAND DREAM PORTAL

We spend over a third of our lives asleep, so a nightstand or bedside table is prime witchcraft-related territory if you ask me. Since you spend A LOT of time next to your nightstand, you should be intentional about curating what goes on it. Whether you want to create space for more purposeful dreaming, keep nightmares away, or just be able to relax into sleep a little easier at night, creating an altar will help! Try to keep clutter to a minimum so your intentionally selected items can have a bigger impact.

Here are some ideas:

HERBAL DREAM POUCH:

Mugwort is my go-to herb for dream support. Within the wider witch world it's an all-time fave. Mugwort adds color and dimension to dreams and encourages lucid dreaming. Its green topside and silvery underside mimic the way the conscious and unconscious mind are two sides of the same coin. One of the easiest ways to work with it is by putting a handful of dried mugwort in a pouch or other container on your nightstand. You could also have a few sprigs in a bud vase (if you don't have cats that love to knock stuff like that over). Throw in a pinch of other herbs like chamomile or lavender to help with relaxation, or valerian and yarrow to clear a path to deep, meaningful dreams.

MUGWORT LINEN SPRAY:

Make an essence of mugwort (see Taurus season), and then add a few drops of your favorite relaxing essential oils. I love a lavender-cedarwood blend. Spray it over your pillows and sheets before lying down to sleep!

CRYSTALS: Whether you use a tumbled stone or two, or a larger crystal cluster is totally up to you. You're working with crystals' specific vibrational frequency, and that will come through in any form (including essences!). I suggest working with something in the blue-purple-white spectrum. Amethyst, celestite, and howlite are my go-tos. The colors connect to your higher energy centers and act as a bridge between the astral plane and the material world. Or, if you have bad dreams or nightmares, a protection stone like black tourmaline or obsidian will attract the negative energy and transmute it before it has a chance to wreck your sleep!

INTENTIONAL PAJAMAS:
Enchant your jammy jams! As we noted in Taurus season's Radical Rest Ritual, never underestimate the power of laundry magick! Plus, it makes doing laundry feel a little less like a chore. Add some moonwater to the washer and some drops of essential oils to dryer balls. In the summer you could even hang pajamas to dry under the moon.

EMPTY NOTEBOOK AND PEN:
It's commonly thought that having a journal and a pen on your nightstand will help you remember your dreams, since you'll be able to write them down right away. I suggest using a specific journal for your dreams rather than a notebook you use for other things. Many witches and dreamwork aficionados will tell you not to pick up your phone before you've recorded your

dreams, but it's the twenty-first century and I use my phone all the time. I spent years with a beautiful notebook on my nightstand and never wrote a word in it. But now, my notes app has a bunch of my dreams (and some other really bizarre stuff) recorded in it.

You can also try to prompt dreams by writing a question or intention and placing it under your pillow.

DIY DREAM DICTIONARY

Whether we go analog or digital for recording our dreams, the trick is to understand the symbolism. Or try to, anyway! Sometimes your house shows up as an ice cream parlor and everyone is throwing ice cream around, and it's just silly and fun. Other times, there are deeper symbols to connect to, which are worth trying to define. Therapists sometimes differentiate between little dreams (like the ice cream example) and big dreams, which carry more subconscious weight. Generally you'll know when you've had one of those. You might wake up feeling shook, or scared, or like you know there's more to the story.

I asked my Jungian analyst what she felt were the most important things to keep in mind when doing dreamwork for healing purposes. Here's what she said:

- Pay attention to how you *feel* when waking up. This links back to intuition and the nexus of thought and feeling. The hidden parts of your mind are trying to communicate, but they don't speak the language of your conscious mind, so in order to understand, you have to connect to the feelings underneath the thoughts.

- The symbols and people in your dreams should be read within the context of your association with them. Dream dictionaries, on the other hand, work on an *objective* level, taking symbols like airplanes, teeth, spiders, and old lovers at face value and implying that they mean the same thing for everyone. But dream decoding should be done on a *subjective* level, within the context of your own experience. For example, an airplane dream to someone like my wife, who loves to travel, will feel very different to someone like me, who hates to fly. Those things should be taken into consideration rather than relying on a dream dictionary or online resource.

It is more effective to consider dreams in their subjective framework and also to keep in mind that everything in a dream relates to an aspect of the dreamer. Even the people! They, including the nice ones, can represent shadow parts of the self. Our shadow self is given a bad rap, but sometimes things that remain in shadow are good! If you struggle with self-esteem, you may not be able to see your good sides clearly, so dreams dress them up in other people. These shadow aspects may show up as an admired friend or trusted loved one, but if you're

dreaming about one of them, it's more about you than the other person. I once had a very simple dream filled with a bunch of my favorite people. My therapist asked me to tell what I loved or admired about them. Then she reassured me that all of these qualities lived inside me too. I just couldn't access a connection to them with my conscious mind (but that's a whole other book, lol . . .).

With all of this in mind, you could aim to make your own dream dictionary, keeping the important symbols that come up within their subjective context. Start by discerning which parts of the dream feel like they hold meaning. If a dead loved one shows up, I would say that's significant. Honestly, people in general, along with pets, places, objects, and goals, all hold meaning. Write them down,

and then add a few key words about what they mean to you in waking life but also how they felt in the dream.

Here's an example related to my dreams about airplanes and travel, topics that for me are related to anxiety, panic, or struggle:

Dad—reassurance, connection
Pools—happiness, freedom, weightlessness, ease
Time—scarcity, pressure, stress
My cat Salem—nurturing, protecting, unconditional love
The end of the world—releasing old patterns

If you can keep up this practice over time, you may end up with an excellent primer for decoding the language of your dreams and connecting to your own inner mysteries!

UPSTREAM OF CONSCIOUSNESS

We have a lot to learn from fish. A school of fish operates based
on something that seems elusive to humans: it's called collective
intelligence. This type of intelligence is a sort of empathetic
understanding of the movements of a group, which makes cooperative
synchronization possible for strategic purposes, such as evading
predators. Put more simply, no one tells the school of fish how to ball
up and move as one entity to protect themselves when a shark swims

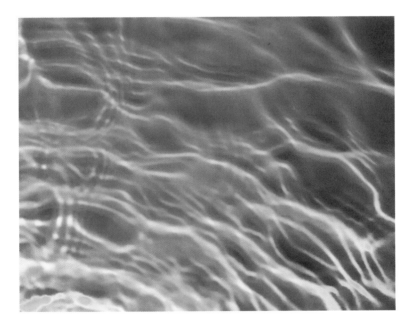

by—they just know they need to do it. It happens effortlessly through a mundane, but also divine, connection.

Could the tools for our collective liberation be inspired by the minds of fish? Or the intuition operating within an anthill or the wisdom of a flock of birds?[2] We all belong to communities, whether or not we feel a connection to those around us. Even if you feel isolated in your world, dozens of people are part of your "school." Of course, your friends, family, and neighbors are there. But let's not forget the people who make our utilities function, who pave the roads we drive on, the people who make our food, take care of the water system, sew our clothes, and in general make our world go around. No matter where you fall on the political or moral spectrum, you still have more in common with these folks than you do with billionaires, nations, governments, or corporations.

And within that same paradigm, we have the power to operate collectively as well, and we must. Poet Emma Lazarus said, "Until we are all free, we are none of us free." If there is one thing that I hope you've gleaned from this book, it is the idea that care is the only way forward. Caring for yourself so that you may then care for and about

2   For more on this topic, *Emergent Strategy* by adrienne maree brown is an excellent resource.

others. It is the only way we will all avoid being eaten alive by the systems of greed and exploitation that are threatening to annihilate all life on earth, and the spirits of nature itself.

So remember, a big fish can swallow a few little fish in one bite. But a bunch of small fish, as a collective, makes an even bigger fish.

THE WORLD IS OURS!

So here we are, at the end of this astrological year! Some people like to think of the zodiac seasons as stages in a human life, starting with brand-new, fresh baby Aries and ending with the wise, elder Pisces. We're a culture obsessed with youth, but think about how much wisdom and experience comes with age. In life we emerge, we grow, we learn, we attach, we build, and we hold. We contemplate, we explore, we appreciate, and we mature. We put it all together, and then we have to learn to let it all go. Pisces represents this willingness to release because it knows that winter always leads to spring.

In tarot, the last card of the Major Arcana is the World. This card represents a finish line of sorts, a job well done, a "You did it!" kind of feeling. But the completion vibes are fleeting. You've grown, you've learned more of the secrets of the universe, but just like our journey through the year, you're not done—in fact you've only just begun! I pulled the World card the day I opened my shop. It was the ending of one huge life cycle and the beginning of a glorious new one. As Paul Quinn says, in *Tarot for Life*:

World consciousness expresses a deep respect for the value of the individual as well as the collective. We begin to take a holistic view of the planet and its inhabitants as integrated, mutually dependent. From there it is a relatively small jump to consider that everything is linked by a greater universal energy—a divine spark—even if that understanding is at first intellectual. Through meditation and contemplation, we take the idea more deeply into the heart, moving us closer to a permanent *knowing,* not a mere believing, that the divine is in us all.

I have to admit, it isn't just the dog videos that have been making me a little weepy. I'm also quite emotional about finishing this book. It has been the honor of my life to write it, and the mix of feelings coming to the surface is deep and, well, *swirly*! There's the relief and pride of finishing what has been one of the biggest projects of my life, but also a little sadness that it's over. I've had so much fun letting my creativity run truly buck-wild, and that is one of the greatest feelings imaginable. I've felt inspired and nourished on a deep and soulful level that I didn't know could exist. One of my hopes for you, dear reader, is that you too can feel as safe to be your most authentic self as I have felt while writing this book.

So, I'm trying not to think about it as an ending; I'm thinking of it as an invitation to respect the nature of cycles. Projects may come to an end, but creativity, curiosity, and ingenuity don't. The end of this book will mean the beginning of something new!

Are you ready? Get your matchbooks out. It's time, once again, to light the primal spark of Aries season!

Further Reading

Abram, David. *Becoming Animal: An Earthly Cosmology*. New York, NY: Vintage Books, 2011.

Battistini, Matilde. *Astrology, Magic, and Alchemy in Art*. Los Angeles, CA: Getty Publications, 2007.

Blum, Amanda. "Kill Your Lawn for Free (and Replace It with Something Better)." Lifehacker, June 27, 2023. https://lifehacker.com/kill-your-lawn-for-free-and-replace-it-with-something-1850575657.

brown, adrienne maree. *Emergent Strategy: Shaping Change, Changing Worlds*. Chico, CA: AK Press, 2017.

———. *Pleasure Activism: The Politics of Feeling Good*. Chico, CA: AK Press, 2019.

Cunningham, Scott. *Magical Aromatherapy*. Woodbury, MN: Llewellyn Publications, 1989.

Cunningham, Scott, and David Harrington. *The Magical Household: Spells and Rituals for the Home*. Woodbury, MN: Llewellyn Publications, 2020.

Davison, Candace. "Leanne Ford Reveals Exactly How You Can Steal Her 'Construction Chic' Style." *House Beautiful*, October 25, 2018. https://www.housebeautiful.com/lifestyle/g24077085/leanne-ford-style/.

De Alberdi, Lita. *Channeling: What It Is and How to Do It*. San Francisco, CA: Red Wheel/Weiser, 2000.

Diaz, Juliet. *Witchery: Embrace the Witch Within*. Carlsbad, CA: Hay House, 2019.

Dickens, Risa, and Amy Torok. *Missing Witches: Recovering True Histories of Feminist Magic*. Berkeley, CA: North Atlantic Books, 2021.

Ducham, Brittany. *Radical Remedies: An Herbalist's Guide to Empowered Self-Care*. Boulder, CO: Roost Books, 2021.

Engelking, Carl. "Hermit Crabs Line Up by Size to Exchange Shells." *Discover* magazine, April 26, 2020. https://www.discovermagazine.com/planet-earth/hermit-crabs-line-up-by-size-to-exchange-shells.

Estés, Clarissa Pinkola. *Women Who Run with the Wolves: Myths and Stories of the Wild Woman Archetype*. New York, NY: Random House, 1997.

Federici, Silvia. *Witches, Witch-Hunting, and Women*. Toronto, ON: Between the Lines, 2018.

Foor, Daniel. *Ancestral Medicine: Rituals for Personal and Family Healing*. Rochester, VT: Bear and Company, 2017.

Friedlander, John, and Gloria Hemsher. *Basic Psychic Development: A User's Guide to Auras, Chakras, and Clairvoyance*. San Francisco, CA: Samuel Weiser, 1999.

Gore, Ariel. *Hexing the Patriarchy: 26 Potions, Spells, and Magical Elixirs to Embolden the Resistance.* New York, NY: Seal Press, 2019.

Gottesdiener, Sarah Faith. *The Moon Book: Lunar Magic to Change Your Life.* New York, NY: St. Martin's Publishing Group, 2020.

Grossman, Pam. *Waking the Witch: Reflections on Women, Magic, and Power.* New York, NY: Gallery Books, 2019.

Halberstam, Judith. *The Queer Art of Failure.* Durham, NC: Duke University Press, 2011.

Hauck, Dennis William. *The Emerald Tablet: Alchemy for Personal Transformation.* New York, NY: Penguin Group, 1999.

Henderson, Raechel. *The Scent of Lemon and Rosemary: Working Domestic Magick with Hestia.* Woodbury, MN: Llewellyn Publications, 2021.

Howe, Rachel. *Healing and Self-Help.* Los Angeles, CA: Small Spells, 2019.

Kaplan, Stuart R. *Artwork and Times of Pamela Colman Smith: Artist of the Rider-Waite Tarot Deck.* Stamford, CT: U.S. Game Systems, 2009.

Karnatz, Jessie Susannah. *Money Magic: Practical Wisdom and Empowering Rituals to Heal Your Finances.* San Francisco, CA: Chronicle Books, 2021.

Kat, Alice Sparkly. *Astrology and Storytelling: Learn Astrology by Writing a Work of Fiction Using Your Natal Chart.* Brooklyn, NY: Self-published, 2020.

———. *Post-Colonial Astrology: Reading the Planets Through Capital, Power, and Labor.* Berkeley, CA: North Atlantic Books, 2021.

Khemsurov, Monica, and Jill Singer. *How to Live with Objects: A Guide to More Meaningful Interiors.* New York, NY: Clarkson Potter, 2022.

Koo, Chaweon. *Spell Bound: A New Witch's Guide to Crafting the Future.* Naarm (Melbourne), Australia: Smith Street Books, 2022.

Lecouteux, Claude. *The Tradition of Household Spirits: Ancestral Lore and Practices.* Rochester, VT: Inner Traditions International, 2013.

Lyons, Sarah. *Revolutionary Witchcraft: A Guide to Magical Activism.* New York, NY: Running Press, 2019.

Mandybur, Jerico. *Rainbow Power: Manifest Your Dream Life with the Creative Magic of Color.* London, UK: Hardie Grant Books, 2022.

Mathis, Lora. "Soft and Radical Realities: Exploring Radical Softness as a Weapon." In *Radical Softness as a Boundless Form of Resistance,* edited by Be Oakley. 5th ed. Brooklyn, NY: GenderFail, 2020.

Mitchell, Larry. *The Faggots and Their Friends Between Revolutions.* Seattle, WA: Calamus Books, 2016.

Nicholas, Chani. *You Were Born for This: Astrology for Radical Self-Acceptance.* New York, NY: HarperCollins, 2020.

Oakley, Be. "Genderfail." GenderFail, 2024. https://genderfailpress.info/.

Oakley, Be, ed. *Radical Softness as a Boundless Form of Resistance.* 5th ed. Brooklyn, NY: GenderFail, 2020.

Odyssey, David. "All About the Age of Aquarius." *Nylon*, September 30, 2022. https://www.nylon.com /life/age-of-aquarius-astrology -explained.

Pivirotto, Nicole. *Color, Form, and Magic: Use the Power of Aesthetics for Creative and Magical Work.* San Francisco, CA: Chronicle Books, 2021.

Pollack, Rachel. *Seventy-Eight Degrees of Wisdom: A Book of Tarot.* San Francisco, CA: Red Wheel/Weiser, 2007.

Progoff, Ira. *Jung's Psychology and Its Social Meaning.* New York, NY: Dialogue House Library, 1985.

Prower, Tomas. *Queer Magic: LGBT+ Spirituality and Culture from Around the World.* Woodbury, MN: Llewellyn Publications, 2021.

Richards, Andrea. *Astrology.* Edited by Jessica Hundley. From *The Library of Esoterica.* Köln, Germany: Taschen, 2021.

Riley, Tess. "Just 100 Companies Responsible for 71% of Global Emissions, Study Says." *The Guardian*, July 10, 2017. https://www.theguardian.com /sustainable-business/2017 /jul/10/100-fossil-fuel-companies -investors-responsible-71-global -emissions-cdp-study-climate -change.

Roux, Avril le. *The Tea Magic Compendium.* Self-published, 2022.

Róisín, Fariha. *Who Is Wellness For? An Examination of Wellness Culture and Who It Leaves Behind.* New York, NY: HarperCollins, 2022.

Schiff, Stacy. *The Witches: Salem, 1692.* New York, NY: Little, Brown and Company, 2015.

Starhawk. *The Spiral Dance: A Rebirth of the Ancient Religion of the Great Goddess.* New York, NY: HarperCollins, 1999.

Tarnas, Richard. *Cosmos and Psyche: Intimations of a New World View.* New York, NY: Plume, 2007.

Thomas, Leah. *The Intersectional Environmentalist: How to Dismantle Systems of Oppression to Protect People + Planet.* New York, NY: Voracious/Little, Brown and Company, 2022.

Torrella, Kenny. "The Case Against Pet Ownership." *Vox*, April 11, 2023. https://www.vox.com/future -perfect/2023/4/11/23673393/pets -dogs-cats-animal-welfare-boredom.

Walton, Agnes, and Kirby Ferguson. "Kill Your Lawn, Before It Kills You." *New York Times*, August 9, 2022. https://www.nytimes .com/2022/08/09/opinion/lawns -water-environment.html.

Yemoonyah, Yamile. *The Seven Types of Spirit Guide: How to Connect and Communicate with Your Cosmic Helpers.* Carlsbad, CA: Hay House, 2020.

Acknowledgments

First, I have to thank my agent, Meg Thompson, for cheerleading me through years of frustration and stagnation until the garden was ready to grow. You've changed my life more than you'll ever know and I'm honored to be your client and friend.

Enormous thanks to my editor, Emma Effinger, for your gentle guidance, kindness, and enthusiasm for this weird little book. To the whole Harvest team, I will always be grateful that you were able to believe in my vision from the very beginning.

Paige Curtin, there's so many things to thank you for I don't even know where to start. Having you as an assistant means I get to laugh and feel supported every single day, but having you as a confidant and collaborator has been the gift of a lifetime. Thank you for all your very tangible help with this book, but also for all our various ventures and adventures together that created the *prima materia* for this project. There's *n-n-n-n-n-n-no way* I could've done it without you.

Christy Czajkowski, thank you for being the best sport, having an amazing imagination, and schlepping an entire dinner picnic through Forsythe Park. Your creativity knows no bounds and I can't wait to see where it takes you next! I trust you will extend my undying gratitude to Junebug and Bat, the true stars of this book.

Jessie Susannah Karnatz, thank you for lending this book a nugget of your genius and magick, the expanse of which I can barely wrap my head around. Thank you in a more general sense for being a Scorpio Rising and a great friend, and for telling me to go for it way back when.

Sailakshmi Ramgopal, your brains and bravery impress me every single day. Thank you for helping me make this book the best and most inclusive version of itself.

Speaking of cheerleaders, Janine Mulone, you are M to the VP. I almost missed my deadline writing this because there's just way too much to say here and I couldn't find the words. (Which you already know because you're usually the person that helps me solve problems like that!) I don't dare even asking the question of where I'd be without you, so just know that I absolutely love being in cahoots with you, *and I'm always saying that.*

Liz Migliorelli, thank you so much for creating Tending the Hearth, which inspired me to explore season-specific intentionality and forever changed my feelings toward winter! The truest gift one can give a New Englander!

To the HausWitch staff: Lish McSweeney, Caroline Holloway, Cole Exley, Denali Musgrave, Kalyn Anderson, Devin Dube, and Dawn Stahura: thank you for holding down the Haus while I worked on this book, and for inspiring it every day along the way.

Morgan Elliott and Jordan Awan, thank you for being so dang cool and creative that I could stand next to you in this life and have some of that coolness wear off on me. Infinite gratitude for once again inviting my readers into your #goals home.

Hendrik Kleinwächter of TheBreadCode, thank you for letting me share your five-thousand-year-old cave bread recipe! You proved (pun intended) so elegantly how four simple ingredients can reveal an important aspect of our shared human experience.

Finally, to my wife, Melissa Nierman, thank you for all the love, healing, tiny breakfasts, and big adventures you've brought into the life I cherish creating with you. I could never be the person who writes books like this if it weren't for you showing me every single day that magick is real.

About the Author

ERICA FELDMANN holds a master's degree in gender and cultural studies, with a research concentration in witches. Her innate interest in the connection between home spaces and wellness led to the creation of HausWitch in 2012.

What started as a "micro budget + magick = makeover" interiors blog would eventually become a thriving online community and brick-and-mortar shop based in downtown Salem, Massachusetts. In 2019, HarperCollins published her book *HausMagick: Transform Your Home with Witchcraft*.

A Gemini Sun, Pisces Moon, and Scorpio Rising, Erica lives with her wife and two cats in the heart of Witch City.